EVERGREEN PILOT BOOKS

Chief Editor
A. Norman Jeffares

Advisory Editors
David Daiches   C. P. Snow

ROBERT GRAVES

ROBERT GRAVES

J. M. Cohen

GROVE PRESS, INC.
NEW YORK

First published by Oliver and Boyd Ltd
Edinburgh, Scotland, 1960

Library of Congress Catalog number 61-6597

First Evergreen Edition 1961

Manufactured in Great Britain

CONTENTS

ACKNOWLEDGMENTS

Thanks are due to Mr Robert Graves for permission to reproduce all quotations from his works made in this book.

Acknowledgments are also due to Messrs A. P. Watt and Son and the following publishers for permission granted in connexion with the works mentioned: Cassell and Co. Ltd. (*Goodbye to All That, Wife to Mr Milton, The Crowning Privilege, The Greek Myths*); Faber and Faber Ltd. (*The White Goddess*); Methuen and Co. Ltd. (*I Claudius, Claudius the God*); Penguin Books Ltd. (*The Greek Myths*).

Acknowledgments are also due to the American publishers of the works indicated: Doubleday and Co. Inc. (*Goodbye to All That, The Crowning Privilege*); Farrar, Straus and Cudahy Inc. (*The White Goddess*); Random House Inc. (*I Claudius, Claudius the God*).

The photograph on the front cover is reproduced by permission of the Radio Times Hulton Picture Library.

I am particularly grateful to Mr Graves for reading this book in typescript and making a number of observations, most of which I have incorporated in the text. Where, therefore, I refer to explanations by Mr Graves without mentioning any published work, these marginal notes are my authority. The poet also set me right on one or two small matters of fact and date, but did not comment on my criticism of his work.

J.M.C

ABBREVIATED TITLES
BY WHICH ROBERT GRAVES'S WORKS
ARE CITED

CHAPTER I

THE POET AT WAR

Robert Graves is a professional writer of great accomplishment in a great number of fields. As an autobiographer and the inventor of a new kind of historical novel he has found his widest public; as a scholar with bold and idiosyncratic theories on myth and religion he has stimulated much controversy. Yet it is as a poet that he ranks highest, and that he is likely to be read by future generations, who may find his other productions no more than entertaining. Graves himself takes this view of his work. In the foreword to his *Poems 1938–45* he baldly proclaimed: "I write poems for poets, and satires or grotesques for wits. For people in general I write prose, and am content that they should be unaware that I do anything else. To write poems for other than poets is wasteful." By writing for people in general, Graves has earned the professional livelihood which has enabled him to continue as a poet. He does not for a moment suggest that even the best of his prose should be placed on the level of the mere 320 pages of his *Collected Poems 1959* by which he wishes to be judged by such of his contemporaries as can be considered poets.

Graves's viewpoint in this matter is exaggerated. In the first place his poetry can be and is appreciated by many who are not practising poets. In the second, some of his prose, in particular his "historical grammar of poetic myth," *The White Goddess*, is so closely connected with his poetry that it cannot be considered on its own. It is my intention, however, as a critic though no poet, to take

Graves's poetry as my subject, and to view his other work as peripheral. My attention will principally be given therefore to the 1959 volume, which contains all those pieces of which he continues to approve. Throughout his life, he has subjected his production to a succession of winnowings. If a poem "happens to be faultily constructed, or written for the wrong reasons," he states in the concluding lines of the foreword to *Poems and Satires 1951*, the poet "will usually recognize this by the way it fades on the page after a few months. The longer one lives and the more poems accumulate, the easier it is to discard doubtful ones."

I believe that Graves has often discarded poems that may, for personal reasons, have faded from his page, but that remain clear and bright in the memory of his readers. I intend therefore to quote as freely from those he has rejected as from those which have survived his final examination. I shall at times also quote in their original version pieces which, having failed to satisfy him, have been altered or rewritten since their first publication. For some poems seem to me to have been undeservedly sacrificed or altered, while others, though inferior to his best, provide useful evidence of his poetic progress, or record journeys up roads that he has never fully explored. As will be shown later, by reference to his own statements, Graves wishes his poems to be considered as a kind of spiritual autobiography or, at least, as an account of a continuous and consequent experience. In fact, however, his work, like that of most other poets, reveals a number of partial explorations, also various changes of direction, all in the course of this single journey, which has led from the Romantic looseness of his war poems of 1914–18 to the close organisation and the deeply pondered and reasoned emotion of his most recent love-poems. Since Graves is, however, anxious that the poems he has discarded shall not be confused with those included in his collected volume, I have starred (*) all quotations from his uncollected work, or from early versions of poems later rewritten.

Robert Graves's place in English poetry is an isolated one. Not only has he never been a member of a school or followed any prevailing fashion, but even in generation he stands alone, too young to have experienced the impact of Continental symbolism which struck W. B. Yeats, T. S. Eliot, and Edwin Muir, and not young enough to have been affected by the social stresses which determined the initial poetic course of W. H. Auden and his group. Though partly Anglo-Irish and partly German by descent, Graves is essentially an English poet. One can find no foreign influence in his work, though he shows some affinities with John Crowe Ransom and others of the American "Fugitive" group. Of his English contemporaries few survived the war with their talents unimpaired. Wilfred Owen and Isaac Rosenberg, both potentially important poets, were killed; and some others who seemed to show promise in 1918 were content, once their war memories had dimmed, to inhabit the minor territories of rural sentiment or private emotion. Theirs has been a small perfection. Graves, on the other hand, though also working on a limited scale, has advanced to become a major poet. To substantiate his claim to this title will be one of the chief purposes of this book.

Robert Graves has proclaimed himself both traditionalist and innovator, Classicist and Romantic by turns. In order to discover his true position in relation to these extremes, I propose to look at a poem typical of his middle period. The twelve-line piece, "Sick Love," which appeared in *Poems 1926–1930* under the title "O Love in Me" is printed with no other change except of punctuation in the 1959 collection. Standing almost half way between Graves's beginnings and his present position, it sufficiently represents his interests, his manner of writing, and his attitude to his subject:

O Love, be fed with apples while you may,
And feel the sun and go in royal array,
A smiling innocent on the heavenly causeway,

Though in what listening horror for the cry
That soars in outer blackness dismally,
The dumb blind beast, the paranoiac fury:

Be warm, enjoy the season, lift your head,
Exquisite in the pulse of tainted blood,
That shivering glory not to be despised.

Take your delight in momentariness,
Walk between dark and dark—a shining space
With the grave's narrowness, though not its peace.

The poem can be thought of as a variation on the old
theme of "Carpe diem"—Love is fleeting; grasp it while
you can. Yet although the poet unhesitatingly advocates
the enjoyment of love while it lasts, he does not consider
this enjoyment an unqualified boon. Already in the third
line irony has crept in. Love is threatened and tainted
from the start; even when self-confidently fed with apples
—and here there may be an implied reference to Eve's
temptation and the Fall—Love is but "a smiling innocent," forever listening for a cry out of the darkness, or
for death in the form of dumb beast or fury. As to the
nature of the taint from which love suffers, it would seem,
by reference to other poems written in the same period
("The Succubus," "Ulysses,"" Down Wanton, Down"),
that it is that of lust. There was also, Mr Graves states, a
taint of madness in the loved woman's heredity. Yet love
remains a "glory." The epithet "shivering" suggests its
hectic nature, and the contradiction in it between heat
and cold.

The poem is ambivalent in its message. Its divided
viewpoint is expressed by the contradictions between the
terzets, and often within the lines also, whereby comfort

alternates with despair, tranquillity with violence. A parallel effect is attained by its broken rhyme pattern, inexact vowel rhymes in the first half being succeeded by equally imperfect consonantal rhymes in the second. But the poem's standpoint is on balance optimistic; love must be accepted although it is from the beginning diseased.

*Midway is man's convenience

is Graves's verdict in another poem, "Midway," written at about the same time. But in other poems of this volume ("Act V, Scene 5," "The Castle") the poet's final judgment is pessimistic. On the whole measured optimism outweighs pessimism in the poet's whole production. It is a chief characteristic with him, however, never to come down whole-heartedly on either side; the purpose of his poem is to present an argument and preserve the suspense of final judgment.

In this sense Graves is related to the Metaphysical school of Donne. The tension in a seventeenth-century poem, however, was not between belief and disbelief, except perhaps in the case of the Spaniard Quevedo, but between different possibilities of belief, mental and emotional. The tension in a Graves poem is, on the contrary, one between heart with its proneness to easy and even sentimental acceptance, and head whose propensity is to deny and to destroy by ratiocination. Robert Graves, who became known while still very young as a minor poet of the first World War, has matured as a major poet of the inner war between emotion and reason, between belief and denial.

In his technique as in his thought Graves has come to take up a half-way position, being neither simple traditionalist nor bold innovator. The language of "Sick Love," beginning with an invocation, seems almost traditional. "Royal array," "smiling innocent," and "heavenly causeway" join noun and epithet in a manner that echoes the Elizabethan, and even recalls Shakespeare. Yet these phrases, while traditionally poetic in themselves, are contrasted with others that are brief, colloquial, and violent. "Listening horror," "the dumb blind beast," "the paranoiac fury" are phrases with a modern immediacy, that make the language of the first terzet appear slightly mocking or pathetic. There is a hint of the contrast so heavily stressed in *The Waste Land* between the ideal world of poetry and the ugliness of actuality. Other phrases like "shivering glory" are tight-packed in the metaphysical manner with possible secondary meanings (hectic glory, glory that shivers with anticipation of its end). The language of the poem in fact becomes more contemporary as it progresses. Yet except for the phrase "paranoiac fury," with its clearly psychoanalytical associations, nothing strikes an aggressively modern note. Truculent modernism was reserved by Graves for those "satires or grotesques" ("Lift Boy," "Repair Shop," etc.) which he was beginning to write "for wits" at the same time as "Sick Love."

Graves has, in latter years, however, come to think of himself as primarily a traditionalist. In his "Preface to a Reading of New Poems at the University of Michigan," published in his miscellany *Steps*,[1] he accepts the title, yet qualifies it by saying that he only does so in so far as he believes that certain principles of poetry cannot be violated without poetry turning into something else. These two main principles on which he takes his stand are the use of a recognisable metre, and "that every word must be given its full meaning." Now though the first has certainly been violated at moments by such important poets as T. S. Eliot, Edith Sitwell, and Dylan Thomas among his contemporaries, none of these poets has consistently neglected rhythmical organisation even to the extent that Whitman did; nor has any poet of eminence used words in the restricted and conventional manner of the eighteenth century, as practised by Beattie, Shenstone, and countless others. Compared with a true contemporary traditionalist, like his friend Edmund Blunden, whose poetry derives from the rural and reflective convention of Cowper, Goldsmith, and Clare, Graves is certainly on the side of the innovators. Indeed in his Michigan address he reminded his audience that in 1927, the year of *The Waste Land*, he wrote in collaboration with Laura Riding *A Survey of Modernist Poetry* (reprinted in his collection of criticisms *The Common Asphodel*)[2] in which he approvingly analysed the work of Gerard Manley Hopkins, T. S. Eliot and, among American poets then completely unknown in Britain, John Crowe Ransom, Hart Crane, and E. E. Cummings. His views on some of these writers, Hopkins and Eliot in particular, have certainly hardened in the last thirty years. In his Clark Lectures of 1954–55, delivered at Cambridge and published as *The Crowning Privilege*, he smothers the poetry of almost all his contemporaries with delightful but not always scrupulously critical invective. It appears that he has lost his taste for other men's poetic experiments. His own work, however, has never become conventional. He continues to stand in his practice on the side of the innovators even though he has come to deny that position. For not only does he not imitate past poets, he consistently avoids the even greater fault of imitating himself. Every Graves poem is a fresh experiment.

Just as Graves stands somewhat to the left of half way between the extremes of traditionalist and innovator, so in the age-old controversy between Classicism and Romanticism, though he has on various occasions changed his standpoint, he has finally taken up an intermediate position nearer to the Classical pole than to the Romantic. His best work of the last ten or fifteen years springs from a moment of Romantic fervour, which is immediately subjected to a Classical or metaphysical process of analysis. He thus arrives at a point too far removed from his initial emotion to count as Romantic, but unlike the pure Classicist who starts from a major poetic theme or commonplace and suppresses the personal link that connects it with his experience, Graves always argues from experience to generalisation.

Graves, like Yeats, began as a full-blooded Romantic. In his essay *On English Poetry* of 1922, he defended the thesis that poetry recording an emotional disturbance or conflict by the Romantic method of self-dramatisation is "true poetry" to the exclusion of all other varieties. But three years later in *Poetic Unreason*, an essay submitted for the Oxford degree of B. Litt. and subsequently printed, he redefined his theory to admit another kind of poetry, to which he gave the name Classical, in which the poet not only recorded his emotional disturbance, but also recognised the allegory which he had unconsciously used to express it. Once he had attained this deeper insight he could then make certain additions and substitutions that would turn his composition into "a solution of one phase at any rate of the conflict." It was at this point that Graves began his practice of standing back from his poem, and treating not only his experience but his own relationship to it as his subject. In the chapter on Secondary Elaboration in *Poetic Unreason*[3] he quotes his early poem "The Bedpost" in two stages of composition, first as a piece of seemingly wayward nonsense, then as he rewrote it three years later after recognising the Freudian significance of its imagery. This recognition was no doubt of value to the poet. But the poem is as fanciful and inconsequent as before, though perhaps rather more deliberate in its fantasy. His explanation that "The shadow of the bedpost is a sexual symbol which the child is not yet physically prepared to recognize"—a symbol which Graves compares to that of the Cross—merely obscures the poem. So long as the bedpost was a fanciful figure that told the child stories it was a charming invention. But once the poet began to attach deeper significances to it, he merely complicated his poem without making it more profound. Imagery that is transparent to the poet loses its efficacy. He must then look for fresh images that continue to hold a charge of emotion for him and preserve their mystery.

"The Bedpost" in its second version endeavours to be a Classical poem possessing two levels of meaning. The psychoanalytical theory of dream-interpretation, from which Graves first adopted his theory of Classicism, may provide a useful weapon for a critic, but is useless to a creator. If he knows his true meaning to lie at a deeper level than his words, then clearly he must set about analysing his experience afresh in new words. A series of prose-explained signs of equivalence (−) will not do. If Keats had understood that La Belle Dame sans Merci represents, as Robert Graves believes, Love, Death by Consumption, and Poetry all at once,[4] then clearly her symbolic figure would have lost most of its force. If the poem had still demanded to be written, it would have been written in a different way. The same is true of "The Bedpost."

Graves's theory, however, is clear-cut. A Romantic poem is a dream vividly and uncritically recorded; a Classical poem not only sets down the dream but interprets at least one of its several meanings. "A modern poet," he wrote,[5] "ought to be an analyst if he wishes his work to last beyond his own generation." On the opening page of the same work he offers a completely psychoanalytical statement of the function of poetry for both writer and reader:

Poetry is for the poet a means of informing himself on many planes simultaneously, the plane of imagery, the intellectual plane, the musical plane of rhythmical structure and texture—of informing himself on these and possibly on other distinguishable planes of the relation in his mind of certain hitherto inharmonious interests or other selves. And for the reader, poetry is a means of similarly informing himself of the relation of

analogous interests hitherto inharmonious on these
same various planes.

Thus a poem is principally important for its curative
value to reader and poet; and in another place Graves
compares an anthology to "a well-stocked medicine chest
against all ordinary mental disorders."[6]

The poet's practice only rarely conformed to these extreme theories. In the beginning, when he made his earliest
impact in the third of Edward Marsh's anthologies,
Georgian Poetry 1916–17, the first of the series to admit the
"war poets," his writing was traditionally Romantic. No
hint of self-consciousness or self-examination occurs in the
eight pieces by which he is represented, of which three
refer to the war, and five belong to his schooldays or the
time of his military training. On the strength of three
war poems, however, he seemed to take his place beside
his friend Siegfried Sassoon, who made his first Georgian
appearance in the same volume.

Graves was at the time of its publication an officer in
the Royal Welch Fusiliers. Having survived the costly
but minor offensives of 1915 and the slaughter of the
Somme in the next year, having been severely wounded,
and invalided home from France after returning there
insufficiently cured of his wound, he was as well qualified
as Sassoon or Wilfred Owen to write poetry of trench
warfare. Yet his war poems arouse no depths of feeling,
and there is little to distinguish those which were written
in anticipation and those that follow his actual initiation
into the muddy and dangerous routines of the Flanders
front. The waste and horror of those years seem to have
struck him with their full force only in retrospect, when
he awoke, as a married man studying at Oxford, to the
fact that most of his generation had failed to return, and
when he began under the burden of a war neurosis to
reproach himself for his undeserved survival.

The poet of *Over the Brazier* (1916) and of the rather

larger *Fairies and Fusiliers* of the next year was a free and
skilful young man who had been writing since the age of
fifteen in a nineteenth-century tradition. Volumes of
Blake and Keats were his companions in the trenches; the
patter of Keats's "Song of Myself"—"There was a
naughty Boy"—and some of Blake's tricks of allegory
have left marks on his earliest work, as have also Hardy
and Housman, Lear, de la Mare, the Border Ballads and
a variety of nursery rhymes and jingles. Perhaps because
of his Irish ancestry, Graves stood a little aside from the
main stream of tradition. At a moment when poetry was
becoming more difficult and self-conscious in its texture,
he wrote loosely with a slapdash mastery of rhyme. "In the
Wilderness," a poem written at school which has been
allowed to survive with only trifling changes in the last
Collected Poems, possesses a captivating ease that Graves
was afterwards at great pains to abandon:

> *Christ of his gentleness
>   Thirsting and hungering,
>   Walked in the wilderness;
>   Soft words of grace He spoke
>   Unto lost desert-folk
>   That listened wondering.
>   He heard the bitterns call
>   From ruined palace wall,
>   Answered them brotherly.

A distant model may be found in "Goblin Market." But
the poem is not a pastiche. It does not exactly catch
Christina Rossetti's measure and it does not echo any of
her lines. The young Graves, in fact, was a literary, week-
end poet, more at home in the nursery and the villages
than some of his more urban and adult fellow Georgians,
and as little inclined as any of them to introduce harsh
thought or strive for compression of line in the way of the
more advanced writers of his time at home and abroad.
"In the Wilderness" is a Romantic and descriptive poem

which perhaps drew its incident from some apocryphal
Bible story. Quite soon, however, and long before he
adopted his theory of multiple levels and secondary intellectual elaboration, Graves began to write poems in a
manner which might be described as Romantically anti-
Romantic. The earliest and best of these, "The Boy in
Church," appeared in *Georgian Poetry 1916–17* in a version slightly different from that printed in *Fairies and
Fusiliers*:

> *The parson's voice runs like a river
>   Over smooth rocks. I like this church.
> The pews are staid, they never shiver,
>   They never bend or sway or lurch.
> 'Prayer,' says the kind voice, 'is a chain
> That draws down Grace from Heaven again.'. . .
>
> It's pleasant here for dreams and thinking,
>   Lolling and letting reason nod,
> With ugly, serious people linking
>   Prayer-chains for a forgiving God.
> But a dumb blast sets the trees swaying
> With furious zeal like madmen praying.

The poem from which these two verses are taken is
marked by a lack of rhetoric rare in a young man. It is
furthermore effortlessly accomplished in its rhythms and
rhyme pattern. Though Georgian in colour, it is not
derivative. Indeed it already shows some signs of the
mature Graves. The poet contrasts two moods, the first
of intellectual impatience, which is heavily stressed in
the opening verses, unquoted, with the parson's words,
manner, and promises, the second of physical satisfaction
with the church's solid structure. Reason protests but
comfortably nods. In the last two lines, however, a third
element, foreboding, is introduced. One is suddenly reminded of the world outside, which at that moment was

a world of war and death, symbolised by the "dumb blast"—the "dumb blind beast" of "Sick Love." In addition another manner of prayer is envisaged, and again there is a parallel with the later poem. The "furious zeal of madmen praying" contains the same thought, less clinically expressed, as "the paranoiac fury." But the turmoil is seen here as an outer disturbance, not as in many of Graves's subsequent poems as a mental conflict. In common with many poets of his time, Boris Pasternak in particular, the early Graves finds the "objective correlative" for his disturbance in the world of nature.

Though assured in rhythm and rhyme, "The Boy in Church" is, like many young men's poems, a little too rich in its adjectives. Graves's subsequent revisions of such early poems as he has preserved concentrate, not unnaturally, on the choice of more precise epithets to replace vaguer and more emotive ones. He also endeavours to strengthen his assonance patterns. He seldom, however, changes his rhymes. The "Boy in Church" speaks of a double expulsion from safety, from the safety of assured beliefs, and from that offered by natural objects, the structure of the church itself. Another poem of the same time hints with somewhat gawky humour at the future irruption of a "Spoilsport," by which Graves symbolises the destructive critical sense that will not only drive him out of the Church, but will also cause him to question even his instinctive reactions to the world of uncertain values that he finds outside:

> *My familiar ghost again
>   Comes to see what he can see,
> Critic, son of Conscious Brain,
>   Spying on our privacy.

The verses are undistinguished, yet they mark the first entrance of a "familiar ghost" that for a long time haunted Graves's poetry.

The first direct response of the young poet to his prospective participation in the fighting was to write some banal and heroic poems in the style of Rupert Brooks. At the same time he strengthened the defences of the childish retreat from which his true inspiration seemed to spring. This was in the first place a world of fantasy with the aid of which he had, perhaps, rendered more bearable life at his particularly philistine public school. There was no actual counterpart for it in his experience. Nevertheless it stood up well to the prospect of battle, and afterwards to battle itself. Mud and shrapnel, at least in anticipation, could be conjured away by the spell of a nursery rhyme:

  *One moment you'll be crouching at your gun
    Traversing, mowing heaps down half in fun:
    The next, you choke and clutch at your right breast—
    No time to think—leave all—and off you go . . .
    To Treasure Island where the Spice winds blow,
    To lovely groves of mango, quince and lime—
    Breathe no good-bye, but ho, for the Red West!
       It's a queer time.

Queerer than the time, however, was the juxtaposition of ideas in the mind of the young officer-poet, lying wounded under morphia in a crater by High Wood on the Somme, to whom death appeared in the guise of a cat that had haunted his childish nightmares. The poem "A Child's Nightmare," though it foreshadows others of the time of his post-war neurosis, has little merit, being careless and conventional in language and crudely hysterical in rhythm. Three lines, however, from its third verse suggest the relationship that he was later to develop between the nursery nonsense that formed his refuge from the crude impact of war and that other nonsense of dreams—in which figures emerged that were more baleful than comforting:

*Nonsense may be light as air,
  But there's Nonsense that can keep
  Horror bristling round the head.

The horror of war, the sounds and smells and jargon of the trenches, the warmth and irritation of life under the shadow of destruction, and the eccentricities of men uprooted from their common world and condemned to a seemingly endless sojourn in limbo, are well recorded in Graves's autobiography, *Good-Bye to All That*, written ten years after the armistice. The graphic quality of this book, which calls up the details of the infantryman's life in France so much more clearly than the more subjective autobiographies of Siegfried Sassoon and Edmund Blunden, proves how indelibly the events and language of trench warfare impressed themselves on Graves's memory. The conversations of his Welsh soldiers are reconstructed with absolute authenticity. Graves records, as never in the poems written in France, the quality of life in that "queer time," obsessive, ugly, and utterly real in its unreality, in which sanity was preserved by occasional vivid flashbacks to the stable world which persisted, the world which he would know again "après la guerre," but which was now temporarily taken over by the politicians, the munition-makers, and all the other enemies of the fighting man. Typical of Graves's vivid prose is a description of Martinpuisch in the Somme area during the early stages of the costly 1916 offensive:

When at last 'D' company reached the trenches, scooped beside a road and not more than three feet deep, the badly shaken Tyneside company we were relieving hurried off, without any of the usual formalities. I asked their officer where the Germans were. He said he didn't know, but pointed vaguely towards Martinpuisch, a mile to our front. Then I asked him who held our left flank, and how far off they were. He didn't know. I damned his soul to Hell as he went away. Having got into touch with 'C' company behind us on the right, and the Fourth Suffolks fifty yards to the left, we began deepening the trenches and presently located the Germans—in a trench-system some five hundred yards to our front, keeping fairly quiet.

The next day at dinnertime, very heavy shelling started: shells bracketed along the trench about five yards short and five yards over, but never quite got it. Three times running, my cup of tea was spilled by the concussion and filled with dirt. I happened to be in a cheerful mood and just laughed. My parcel of kippers from home seemed far more important than any bombardment—I recalled with appreciation one of my mother's sayings: 'Children, remember this when you eat your kippers; kippers are cheap, yet if they cost a hundred guineas each they would still find buyers among the millionaires.'[7]

By contrast "The Leveller," a discarded poem written at the time, which narrates an incident in an attack near this place a few days later, opens conventionally, "Near Martinpuisch that night of hell," and is made up of little more than clichés. The best poem that Graves wrote in France was the story of the ghostly soldier "Corporal Stare," who passed by the window of a house in Béthune in which Graves and some fellow officers were dining, although actually killed a month before at Festubert. Though told in a light-hearted way, this poem already foreshadows the more intensely haunted ghost poems of the *Pier Glass* volume of 1921. Graves narrates the incident again and more circumstantially in *Good-Bye to All That*.[8] France was, as he remembers, full of ghosts at that time.

Early in 1917 Graves was invalided home to spend the remaining eighteen months of the war in various training and administrative posts in the British Isles. He was therefore spared the ordeal of his friend Siegfried Sassoon, who publicly declared himself against the war, refused to fight again, and invited a court martial. Graves, like many of his fellow officers, had come to disbelieve in the justice of the war, but argued that "everyone was mad except ourselves and one or two others, and that no good could come of offering common sense to the insane. Our only possible course would be to keep on going until we got killed."[9] Graves also pointed out that it would be impossible for Sassoon to make the men of their battalions understand his point of view. Sassoon refused to agree. But Graves and other friends were able to prevent the court martial and to see that Sassoon was called before a medical board. In giving evidence on his friend's behalf before this board, Graves himself wept three times.[10] Sassoon was finally persuaded to submit himself to psychological treatment at the pioneer hospital at Craiglockhart, and while staying there wrote the devastating series of poems afterwards published in his volume *Counter Attack*. Nevertheless after a few months, though unfit for service and still holding the same views as before, he volunteered to fight again. Feeling for the men he had led was stronger than his indignation against the politicians' war.

At Craiglockhart Sassoon came under the care of Professor W. H. R. Rivers, a Cambridge neurologist and anthropologist, who was beginning to practise the Freudian method of dream interpretation in a modified form and who was later to exert a great influence on Graves also.

While serving with a cadet battalion which was training fresh officers to replace the heavy casualties of the 1917 offensives, Graves wrote the poems of his next volume, *Country Sentiment*, which he described in *Good-Bye to All That*[11] as "a book of romantic poems and ballads." The best piece that he had so far written in this vein was the somewhat clumsy "Double Red Daisies," which appeared in a number of anthologies, and was therefore soon discarded for its easy popularity. The best of *Country Sentiment* is technically more accomplished. Graves had

learnt to use ballad metre as effortlessly as A. E. Housman.
The density of the poems is, however, uneven. Super-
ficially none of them appear to refer to the war. All belong
to that nursery world of refuge in which Graves had
acquired an additional stake by marriage and the birth
of his first child. As a whole, *Country Sentiment* succeeds in
keeping the war at bay. Some of the pieces are on a very
light level. "A Song for Two Children," for example, presents no problems and hints at no underlying meanings.
It is a pure medley of nursery rhymes which, as he tells us,
suffered a sharp rhythmical change half-way through its
composition, owing to the arrival of a military band
beneath the window at which he was writing.[12] The
beautiful "Apples and Water," on the other hand, is as
much concerned with "the pity of war" as any of Graves's
overt war-poems. A daughter takes pity on some passing
soldiers and wishes to quench their thirst. But her mother
restrains her, for she herself has quenched a soldier's
thirst in some earlier war. The burden of the poem seems
to be, that wars are eternally recurrent, and that soldiers
and women suffer in them alike. "Apples and Honey"
has undergone revision, and the harshness of its anecdote
has been somewhat toned down. In the original version
the soldiers "march away to die," and the soldier on
whom the mother took pity appears to be the girl's
father. The later rendering ends on a more generalised
note of sorrow, voiced by the mother:

> There is no water can supply them
>   In western streams that flow;
> There is no fruit can satisfy them
>   On orchard trees that grow.
>
> Once in my youth I gave, poor fool,
>   A soldier apples and water;
> And may I die before you cool
>   Such drouth as his, my daughter.

Again in a poem of still greater intensity, "Outlaws," which has also undergone revision, the theme of evil, connected with memories of the pagan gods, almost certainly carries some secondary reference to the war. However, the poet had perhaps already realised in the light of Rivers's theories that powers of destruction lay in wait not only in the woods of the Somme but also in the depths of a man's own mind.

> Old gods, tamed to silence, there
>   In the wet woods they lurk,
> Greedy of human stuff to snare
>   In nets of murk.

These silent survivors from the pagan world, standing for both mental and physical menaces, are not however to Graves uncompromisingly hostile. He has always been on the side of the old gods, in whose realm he believed the springs of poetry to lie. What they bring is a complete reversal of values. The next verse of "Outlaws" in fact suggests the theme of "through the looking glass" which he was later to treat more thoroughly in such poems as "Alice" and "The Terraced Valley":

> Look up, else your eyes must drown
>   In a moving sea of black;
> Between the tree-tops, upside down,
>   Goes the sky track.

Graves's world was at this time an upside-down world in which, as he stated some years later in his "Song of Contrariety":

> Far away is close at hand,
>   Close joined is far away.

The war, just over when he was writing these, his first cryptic poems, was in his thoughts close at hand, while that which was most closely joined to him, his love of wife and children, was an elusive thing, easily expelled by the memory of war.

What remained most constant was a landscape, the landscape of that country near Harlech where Graves had purchased a cottage in the worst moments of the war in order to have some physical foothold in the other world at peace. This moorland stretching back from the dunes to the trackless, unspoiled Rhinogs represented for him a tract of country outside time and hardly affected by changes of season. It was a territory haunted by half-forgotten predatory creatures, "the first land that rose from Chaos and the Flood," and here the old gods still walked through their creeds had long "whirled away." Again we can see that concern with the old religion that was to distinguish the author of *The White Goddess*.

In revising "Rocky Acres," the outstanding poem in the collection, for the 1938 *Collected Poems*, Graves made fewer changes than in "Outlaws." He merely removed a few superfluous adjectives, and occasionally substituted the more precise for the looser and more evocative, thus rendering the poem's abrupt rhythms even more staccato:

> Time has never journeyed to this lost land,
> Crakeberry and heather bloom out of date,
> The rocks jut, the streams flow singing on either hand,
> Careless if the season be early or late,
> The skies wander overhead, now blue, now slate;
> Winter would be known by his cutting snow
> If June did not borrow his armour also.
> Yet this is my country, beloved by me best,
> The first land that rose from Chaos and the Flood,
> Nursing no valleys for comfort and rest,
> Trampled by no shod hooves, bought with no blood.
> Sempiternal country whose barrows have stood
> Stronghold for demigods when on earth they go,
> Terror for fat gurghers on far plains below.

This land, like that of Graves's nursery rhymes, is a refuge outside time that has resisted the invasions and depredations of man. It is also a base for retaliatory raids

on the "fat burghers" of the valleys, who clearly bear
some relationship to the "hard-faced men who looked as if
they had done pretty well out of the war," who were the
butts of Sassoon's satires, and were ruling post-war England. The demi-gods or "outlaws" who increasingly haunt
Graves's poetry in a number of forms—trolls, ogres, and
lollocks—embody his desire to return into an innocent
past, which he has hitherto thought of as the world of
childhood, but they also express his contempt, which was
not present in his nursery rhymes, for the commonplace,
the cruel, and the uninspired. The old gods have retired,
but they will strike back with all the force of nightmare
once darkness has fallen, and the poets will be on their
side.

As a defender of the old gods and enemy of the "burghers," Graves was now moving into literary opposition.
Although he contributed to the Georgians' periodical,
The London Mercury, he had now become an anti-Georgian.
1920 was no year for the avant-garde, and it was not till
three years later that he contributed, under the pseudonym of John Doyle, to the new and radical *Calendar
of Modern Letters* his Skeltonic manifesto, "The Marmosite's Miscellany," in which he pilloried the Georgian
school of poetry in the person of Edward Marsh, who had
first introduced him to a wider public. Marsh and the
poets of the *Mercury* were, as Graves now saw it, "poised
on the edge of a sofa . . . between the soft cushions of
tradition and the hard floor of modernism."[13]

In "Rocky Acres" the twenty-four-year-old poet came
down to this "hard floor." Here for the first time we have
his true manner, authentic in its rejection of all embel-
lishment and as deliberately ponderous and reflective in
its assonances as the ballads beside which it appeared
were easy and decorative. If "Apples and Water" represents the height of Graves's achievement in his old manner, "Rocky Acres" shows not only promise but positive
achievement in his new.

"Rocky Acres" owes something of its deliberately awkward style, its irregular accentuation and its earthy language to the example of John Skelton. Graves had been experimenting with Skeltonic metres for perhaps four years; and here he attempted the rhyme royal, a seven-line stanza used by Chaucer and his successors, also by Skelton himself in his elegy on the Earl of Northumberland. Graves however does not follow the rigid metrical pattern of the old measure. He had clung more closely to his model in a set of Skeltonics in honour of that long unread and unhonoured master, which appeared in *Fairies and Fusiliers*:

> *For he will not stop
> To sweep nor mop,
> To prune nor prop,
> To cut each phrase up
> Like beef when we sup,
> Nor sip at each line
> As at brandy-wine,
> Or port when we dine.

Graves certainly admired Skelton's apparent facility and the ease and truculence of his rhymes. Though he too achieved an appearance of spontaneity, each of his poems cost him the labour of four or five versions. But he learnt more from Skelton than a mere lesson in poetic agility. In this Tudor poet he found the link with the older, accentual types of English verse, which most of his contemporaries were trying to establish.

All the chief poets of the post-war era attempted to escape from the bondage of the outworn iambic line, and the chief alternative in the English tradition was that accentual poetry which fell out of polite usage with the Renaissance. Gerard Manley Hopkins worked out the formula afresh under the name of "sprung rhythm." But temperamentally, "poor tortured" Hopkins and Graves stood very far apart. Religious tension has never played any part in Graves's poetry or thought; the asceticism which made the Jesuit poet "bite his nails to the quick" was indeed abhorrent to Graves.[14] Nor had he, fundamentally, any greater sympathy with Yeats, Ezra Pound, or Eliot, though he was prepared to act as their advocate against the reactionary critics.[15] Among the experimentalists of his generation only Wilfred Owen was congenial to him. But Owen's alliterative technique, though no doubt fully developed in his unfinished masterpiece "Strange Meeting," did not give Graves the lead he required. In seeking an ancestry and exemplars for the kind of poetry that he wished to write, he therefore looked back to Skelton, and behind him to generations of popular poets, Middle English, Saxon, Welsh, and Irish, who had recognised before him that "regular verse, though a wonderful aid to memory, is soporific unless frequent changes occur in the metre.[16]

"Rocky Acres" is derived far less directly from the rediscovered accentual tradition than certain early poems in W. H. Auden's first volume. It is, however, Graves's first poem in his developed style, and the example of Skelton was the force that gave him final freedom from the tight iambic convention. Total freedom, however, Graves did not desire. When naming the few real poets who survived into his life-time, he listed not only Wilfred Owen but Hardy and W. H. Davies.[17] These two represented for him not freedom but discipline. Graves had already a sense of obligation to the intelligent "reader over his shoulder," whom some of the modernist poets despised. He felt it necessary to make plain statements, or at least statements that could be expanded and justified in prose. He had also a predilection for visual accuracy. The flight and eating habits of the buzzard are as exactly noted in "Rocky Acres" as in an ornithological essay:

> He soars and he hovers, rocking on his wings,
> He scans his wide parish with a sharp eye,

He catches the trembling of small hidden things,
He tears them in pieces, dropping from the sky.

The rocking of the bird's flight too is admirably con-
veyed by the irregular accentuation of the verse, in which
nothing but the rhyme is constant. For, thanks to the
Skeltonic influence, neither syllable-count nor alliterative
pattern is regular and the strong caesura falls variously
from line to line.

The course that Graves appears now to have set himself was towards increasing accuracy of vision and complexity of thought, expressed in the simplest and most
economical way. He was addicted to no special vocabulary; he drew on the full resources of language. The
general tendency of poetry both at home and on the
Continent was, however, towards a greater complexity,
and even opacity, of language. Here Graves stood apart.
In "Rocky Acres" he drew a landscape and related it to a
state of mind, a device practised by modern poets as
various as Rilke, Edwin Muir, Boris Pasternak, and W. H.
Auden. But in contradistinction to them all he made his
landscape as vivid as his self-anatomy, thus standing in
this particular also half-way between the opposite poles
of Romanticism and Classicism, traditionalism and
innovation.

REFERENCES

1. *Steps*, pp. 236–7.
2. *The Common Asphodel*, pp. 61–167.
3. *Poetic Unreason*, pp. 104–9.
4. *The White Goddess*, p. 429.
5. *P.U.*, p. 82.
6. *P.U.*, p. 2.
7. *Good-bye to All That*, p. 176.
8. *G.B.*, p. 102.
9. *G.B.*, p. 215.
10. *G.B.*, p. 216.
11. *G.B.*, p. 228.
12. *G.B.*, pp. 229–30.
13. *Collected Poems, 1914–26*, p. 198, note.
14. *The Crowning Privilege*, pp. 127 and 157.
15. *C.A.*, pp. 61–167, passim.
16. *Cr. Pr.*, p. 107.
17. *Cr. Pr.*, p. 133.

CHAPTER II

THE SURVIVING GHOST

Graves tells the story of his immediate post-war years in his autobiography.[1] Going up to Oxford five years late, he read fitfully for an English degree, living with his wife and children in a cottage on Boars Hill rented them by John Masefield, who admired his poetry. Later he moved to a cottage at Islip. During this time there was much domestic work to be done, and there was also a brief experiment in shopkeeping. Graves received generous help from many friends and fellow writers, and pursued the writing of poetry as his principal activity. He wanted neither job nor profession.

From 1920 to 1923, the prevailing mood of Robert Graves's poetry was, in the words of his prefatory note to the collection *Whipperginny*, "aggressive and disciplinary": aggressive towards the unintelligent reading public, whom he now made no attempt to please, and disciplinary in regard to himself in so far as he now saw his writing as at least in part a curative technique with which to master and clear up his war neurosis. He was under the necessity of laying the ghosts not only of his comrades who had died in the war but of his own self-reproach for having survived. The theme is adumbrated in the brief poem "Haunted," which appeared at the end of *Country Sentiment*:

> *I meet you suddenly down the street,
>   Strangers assume your phantom faces,
>   You grin at me from daylight places,

> Dead, long dead, I'm ashamed to greet
> Dead men down the morning street.

Graves recounts encounters of this sort in the streets of Oxford; there were for him and for others moments in which the trench-lines under bombardment were more real than the city outside the lecture-room windows.[2] The theme of haunting had already, as has been noted, occurred in the poem "Corporal Stare," written when he was in France; and *Good-Bye to All That* contains more than one story of ghosts met on the battlefield. But now the experiences of his first months in France had become obsessive. They did not finally leave him until well into 1928.[3] The way in which they recurred is recorded in a short poem called "The Occasion," which is dated 1920:

> *"The trenches are filled in, the houseless dead
> Disperse and on the rising thunder-storm
> Cast their weak limbs, are whirled up overhead
> In clouds of fear . . ."
>   Then suddenly as you read,
> As we sat listening there, and cushioned warm,
> War-scarred yet safe, alive beyond all doubt,
> The blundering gale outside faltered, stood still:
> Two bolts clicked at the glass doors, and a shrill
> Impetuous gust of wind blew in with a shout,
> Fluttering your poems. And the lamp went out.

This poem, which records an incident that occurred at Sassoon's house, repeats the image of the "dumb blast" of "Boy in Church." Poem and sermon, warm cushioned room and quiet church interior, are alike invaded by the harsh wind of the world outside.

Despite Graves's claim that he did not set out to please his public, nor yet to "confer benefits upon posterity"[4] the poems of his next volume, *The Pier Glass*, present few obscurities. Such as do occur seem to spring rather from his inability to work out a dream image satisfactorily than from any impatience with the task of plain communication. The charge of emotion in this volume of 1921 is on a level with that of the best poems in *Country Sentiment*. Technically, on the other hand, containing as it does no piece as accomplished as "Rocky Acres," it marks no advance. The title poem, in which he returns to the iambic pentameter, is a highly concentrated study of a haunting by a living woman, who walks like a ghost every night through the "lost manor" of Maesynenardd, near Harlech, up a "broad stair" to a "huge bed of state," the occupant of which one is to suppose she murdered. But the anecdote is mysterious, and in the collected edition the poem now appears in truncated form. The ending, in which some resolution was attempted, has been cut away; and the woman is left praying before a mirror for assurance that somewhere there exists an alternative to the haunted life she is leading:

> The windows frame a prospect of cold skies
> Half-merged with sea, as at the first creation,
> Abstract, confusing welter. Face about,
> Peer rather in the glass once more, take note
> Of self, the grey lips and long hair dishevelled,
> Sleep-staring eyes. Ah, mirror, for Christ's love
> Give me one token that there still abides
> Remote, beyond this island mystery,
> So be it only this side Hope, somewhere,
> In streams, on sun-warm mountain pasturage,
> True life, natural breath; not this phantasma.

The passage conveys a disordered sense of urgency by means of a dispersion of accents recalling that of "Rocky Acres" though less noticeable in these blank verse lines than in the rhyme royal of the earlier poem. But the nature of the "island mystery" remains unexplained. Since the woman addresses the poet, speaking of "your broad stairs," and claiming to be

Drawn by a thread of time-sunk memory,

which must also be the poet's, she might seem to have
become the figure of a dream, which arises from the
depths of his memory. The message of this dream seems
to be that, whether looking outwards through the window at the inchoate welter of sky and sea, or at the cracked
pier glass inside, the woman or poet can find no comfort.
Yet it is to the sullen glass that she prays for hope. Not
wild nature, as is suggested in "Rocky Acres", but a dis-
torted reflection of one's true self contains the secret comfort which releases one from the "island" of personal
isolation on which one is imprisoned.

This interpretation may explain some of the poem's
obscurities; it is clearly concerned with the idea of release from guilt. But unlike "The Bedpost," "The Pier
Glass" has failed to communicate the secret of its imagery
even to the poet.

The poem's suppressed conclusion leads to a half-
resolution, from which it turns away. Things will be as
they were; there is no release. The symbol of order and
sanity, the sound of bees swarming (as they did at
Maesynenarrd) between the mirror and the outer wall—
and by implication in a deeper level of the poet's mind
than that of his dream—confronts him with a judgment
and a possibility of atoning for the past. Presented with
the alternative, "Kill or forgive," the murderess obsti-
nately decides:

Kill, strike the blow again, spite what shall come.

and the bees take up the refrain. The neurosis in fact
triumphs, making common sense or deeper insight sing
chorus to its tune. The question has been put again "out
of due time for fresh deliberation," and the answer is no
more pleasing than before to "the Master's ear." Yet in
the cancelled lines which set out to give the prayed-for
token of hope there is an assurance which the poem

suffers by losing:

> *   death prevails not yet.
> For bees have swarmed behind in a close place
> Pent up between this glass and the outer wall.
> The combs are founded, the queen rules her court,
> Bee-sergeants posted at the entrance chink
> Are sampling each returning honey-cargo
> With scrutinizing mouth and commentary,
> Slow approbation, quick dissatisfaction.
> Disquieting rhythm, that leads me home at last
> From labyrinthine wandering.

The passage is imperfectly worked out. The bees, who in their orderliness and their "sampling of each returning honey-cargo" seem to stand for some apprehension of truth capable of leading the poet home "from labyrinthine wandering," are yet swayed by the judgment of the woman whose face is reflected in the mirror. A question has been put and the wrong solution has been found; and death appears once more to prevail.

A constant theme in the slighter poems in the *Pier Glass* collection is one of self-reproach for guilt incurred in childhood by some unknown wrongdoing:

> *Why do you spell 'untrue, unkind,'
>   Reproachful eyes plaguing my sleep?
> I am not guilty in my mind
>   Of aught would make you weep. . . .
> The black trees shudder, dropping snow,
>   The stars tumble and spin.
> Speak, speak, or how may a child know
>   His ancestral sin?

Seldom, however, does the poet's state of tension seem to be as acute as in "The Pier Glass." Sometimes he appears to accept it as a necessary ingredient of the creative power. The hyperaesthesia described in the poem "Lost Love," which contains some distant echoes

of Ralph Hodgson's "Song of Honour," is accepted for
its enhancement of the power of vision. The poet who
has lost his love comes into closer relationship with
nature:

> His eyes are quickened so with grief,
> He can watch a grass or leaf
> Every instant grow; he can
> Clearly through a flint wall see,
> Or watch the startled spirit flee
> From the throat of a dead man.

Loss of love, or the loss of the power to love, is a
principal theme of the *Pier Glass* volume. The guilty man,
or persistent murderess, whom Graves finds in himself,
has a fascination for him. In the unsuccessful and quickly
discarded poem "Distant Smoke," the sons of Seth for-
feit Adam's dying benediction by wandering into the
desert in search of "this monster, a new man," who is the
son of the first murderer Cain. The poet seems here to
take the side of the obstinate rebel once more, as in "The
Pier Glass," and willingly, in the name of Seth's sons, to
shoulder his burden of guilt.

In the powerful poem of insomnia "Down," the poet
appears hopelessly to be seeking an escape from brooding
nightmare by a return to childhood:

> Oh, to be a child once more, sprawling at ease
> On smooth turf of a ruined castle court!

But there is no ease in this memory of childhood. For the
child had already been experimenting with the world of
darkness by dropping stones into the "secret void" of an
ancient well, and then lying

> As if unborn, until life floated back
> From the deep waters.

In childhood there had been free communication
between these depths of the uncharted mind and "the

towering sky." But for the sick and sleepless man who is first described and then allowed to sleep, there is no such return. Somehow, inadvertently he had destroyed himself:

> there was some word uttered,
> Some abracadabra—then, like a stage-ghost,
> Funereally with weeping, down, drowned, lost!

Graves appears to be speculating on the problem of original sin which, in another poem, "Children of Darkness," he refers back to the moment in which the children demand to be born:

> We spurred our parents to the kiss,
> Though doubtfully they shrank from this—
> Day had no courage to pursue
> What lusty dark alone might do:
> Then were we joined from their caress
> In heat of midnight, one from two.

Hence it is that, conceived as children of darkness, who knew no discontent before our birth,

> We loathe to gaze upon the sun.

The pessimistic burden of these poems seems almost to be that "not to have been born is best."

But the poet's desire to escape from the insomniac world of "half-riddles, answerless" was extremely strong. In the somewhat confused dream-legend "The Gnat" he envisaged the prospect of ridding himself of his incubus even at the cost of sacrificing his powers of creation. He is willing that the one self, the shepherd Watkin who heard the inner voice, shall die, leaving the other, the labourer Watkin, to survive. As for the shepherd,

> *Oh, he's forgotten. A dead dream, a cloud.
> Labourer Watkin delves, drowsily, numbly,
> His harsh spade grates among the buried stones.

There are several poems in the book, however, that tell of the poet's survival, and even foreshadow the claims to be made for his magical prowess in "Virgil the Sorcerer." In "The Troll's Nosegay" he is presented as a demi-god who conjures up "a bunch fit to amaze a China Queen" for a lady whose demand had only been for a simple nosegay out of season.

Something near to a resolution is reached in "Return," in which the poet proclaims that "the seven years' curse is ended," and after threatening to transfer his punishment to an alter ego of "cold, malicious brain and most uncharitable, cold heart" succeeds in forgiving his scapegoat, sending him off to

> disgrace
> Some other green and happy place

while he himself returns to the natural landscape that he had drawn, not seven but perhaps three years before, in "Rocky Acres."

A more complete resolution is reached, however, in "The Stake," which tells of the birth from the heart of a suicide buried at the cross-roads, of a new shoot, "neither ill nor very fair, neither Rose nor Upas," but

> *A green-tufted oak-tree
> On the green wold,
> Careless as the dead heart
> That the roots enfold.

The guilt or innocence of the suicide matter nothing. "Spring calls, and the stake answers"; it is as simple as that.

The *Pier Glass* volume records a crisis in the poet's life, the aftermath of his war experience. Dreams, haunting and metaphysical speculation, at times made excessive demands on the poet's powers of expression. At times he lost his way, bewildered by a half-understood vision that he could not reduce to order. But the poems even in their obscure passages have a Romantic strength; and it is almost with disappointment that one reads in this ghost-haunted collection a poem of such easy feeling as "The Patchwork Bonnet," which was rooted in the family life at Islip that Graves describes in his autobiography. This piece, like "Double-Red Daisies," later incurred his dislike for appearing in too many anthologies, and does not survive in his *Collected Poems*. Though to some extent a hangover from his early ways of writing, it testifies to the continued existence, despite neurosis and psychoanalytical burrowings, of a poet of direct vision and simplicity.

Haunted life and cottage life alike were ceasing to provide adequate subjects for Graves's poetry. The disorder revealed in "The Pier Glass" and partially resolved in "The Stake" began to yield to intellectual speculation. Romanticism was succeeded by a new Classicism, involving not so much self-examination as the consideration of a given case. Graves's next volume, *Whipperginny* of 1923, contains some Romantic poems, but it was the debate between head and heart that now principally occupied the poet's attention. No more myths being supplied by nightmare, he began to exercise a new inventiveness in contriving his anecdotes. "The Lord Chamberlain tells of a Famous Meeting," "Richard Roe and John Doe," and "An Idyll of Old Age" introduce his new poetry of ironic hypothesis—Consider this case or this. The prevailing note of *Whipperginny* is, in the words of its preface, "the appearance of a new series of problems in religion, psychology and philosophy, no less exciting than their predecessors, but, it may be said, of less emotional intensity." The greater strictness of his writing, however, now laid the poet open to "accusations of trying to get publicity and increase his sales by a wilful clowning modernism."[5]

The Lord Chamberlain tells of the meeting of the two princes of East and West, each in disguise, "over a ragged pack of cards" at a soldier's mess in the camp of the Middle Kingdom. Annalists, biographers, essayists, dramatists, and allegorical painters have each given their highly embellished accounts of this famous event; the Chamberlain, however, who was present with his master, the prince of the East Kingdom, tells a tale of modest restraint; there were no dramatic happenings; there was no miraculous juggling with the cards. Each prince displayed his greatness and his consciousness of the historic occasion by a gesture, which the Chamberlain describes in very plain language:

> *One thing is true, that of all sights I have seen
> In any quarter of this world of men,
> By night, by day, in court, field, tavern, or barn,
> That was the noblest, East encountering West,
> Their silent understanding and restraint,
> Meeting and parting like the Kings they were
> With plain indifference to all circumstance;
> Saying no good-bye, no handclasp and no tears,
> But letting speech between them fade away,
> In casual murmurs and half compliments,
> East sauntering out for fresh intelligence,
> And West shuffling away, not looking back;
> Though each knew well that this chance meeting stood
> For turning movement of world history.
> And I? I trembled, knowing these things must be.

All Romantic implications are denied; there was "no good-bye, no handclasp and no tears." Yet the poem gains most of its colour by the exposition of just these Romantic hypotheses, and furthermore this meeting was, as the Chamberlain knew, despite its lack of drama indeed "a turning movement of world history."

It is impossible to account for Graves's omission of this magnificent poem from his winnowed collection. Built up in deftly conversational verse out of a series of negations—"Never believe approved biographers"—"Neither believe those elegant essayists"—"Also distrust those allegorical painters," etc.; denying all divine interference

and lauding the most reticent "human splendour," it
builds up to the climax of its conclusion, just quoted,
patiently step by step. It is Graves's most sustained poem,
the longer "Marmosite's Miscellany" lacking, as its name
implies, any real unity; and it will bear comparison with
a dramatic idyll by Browning or Robert Frost. It is in
fact close to the American manner; and it is at this point
that Graves seems first to have been impressed by the
conversational flatness used by Frost and others on the
other side of the Atlantic.

Graves's Romantic anti-Romanticism, first attempted
in "The Boy in Church," and perfected in the framework of a Classical anecdote in "The Lord Chamberlain,"
is less successful, because more crudely ironic, in "An
Idyll of Old Age." For the bedside conversation of the
aged lovers Baucis and Philemon is palpably absurd.
Though their guests Zeus and Hermes, who lie in the
adjacent room, may be deceived by their apparent
generosity in offering one another freedom to break the
marriage vow, this is only because

> *Eternal Gods deny the sense of humour.

In fact the time for such gestures has long since passed.
The Gods may complacently affirm that in truth

> Neither would faithless to the other be,
> Would not and could not, being twined together
> In such close love that he for want of her
> Removed one night-time from his side would perish,
> And she was magnet-drawn by his least wish.

But the poet knows that in fact neither lover has the freedom to stray. This "idyll overheard" rehearses only
"remembered conflicts"; one of the lovers is now palsied,
the other impotent.

These last two poems set out and explode hypotheses
in the interests of a reality which is undramatic in the
first, and in the second absurd. In "Richard Roe and

John Doe" also flamboyant gestures are laughed out of court; the cuckolded Roe may wish himself Job, Solomon, or Alexander the better to bear his humiliation, but what he wishes most of all is still to enjoy his wife, in fact to be John Doe.

The last only of these poems continues to have the poet's approval. He has been particularly severe with his writing of this period, which produced many fine pieces that seemingly appeared to him later to be foreign to his proper line of development. A number of patently Romantic poems have been sacrificed also, among them one, "The Rock Below," which gives a symbolic account of the stages of his recovery from his war neurosis and comes to a triumphant conclusion with the introduction of the image of the phoenix tree. "A muttering from the earth" demands that the weeds be cleared from the poet's land. Under the weeds are thorn-stocks, and these too are wrenched out. But the rose-tree that the poet plants will not grow, for its roots are on the rock. Then the poet labours with the rock itself, which he succeeds in breaking, and the last verse tells of a miracle:

> *Now from the deep and frightful pit
>   Shoots forth the spiring phoenix tree
> Long despaired in this bleak land,
> Holds the air with boughs, with bland
>   Fragrance welcome to the bee,
>   With fruits of immortality.

But the mature Graves will not allow himself such fruits; the word immortality is suspect to him. He even insists that his writing is for his own generation, and refuses to appeal to posterity. Moreover the stream of his poetic creation had now to take another turn into more arid country. The triumph of his emergence from nightmare was premature. When he announced it even more loudly in "The Ridge Top," he struck a false note. The poem begins with the accurate memory of a mountain walk, only to end with the characterless portrayal of a companion who from woman has been transformed into a conventional symbol.

The spiring phoenix-tree was indeed not ready to shoot forth. The thorn-stocks were, however, already almost uprooted. In this volume appears somewhat belatedly the second version of "The Bedpost," which has survived to the last, whereas not only "The Chamberlain" but "The Rock Below" have been purged.

The one consistent note in *Whipperginny* is a lament for the loss of pure emotion. Love is no longer a simple feeling, as it was assumed to be in the nursery-rhyme poems; and to evoke it as a force capable of conjuring away "dream despair" is to lose it instantly:

> *Is the presence empty air,
>   Is the spectre clay,
> That Love, lent substance by despair,
> Wanes, and leaves you lonely there
>   On the bridal day?

In the later version of this "Song of Contrariety" the evocative word *presence*—surely the proper alternative to *spectre*—is replaced by the more concrete *person*. "Dream despair" may arise from the absence of love or the unreality of the loved one. It may also arise from the unresolved battle between yea and nay. "Old Wives' Tales" tells that outer fears are really only the projection of inner fears; and a more powerful poem, "The Avengers," attributes the cause of this battle to the grafting of inconsistent elements on to man's nature at his birth. "Western May" struggles with "Northern briar," "mistletoe" fights "against green things of South and East," and the poet can see no possibility of a resolution:

> *For bloom of quince yet caps the may,
>   The briar is held by Sharon's rose,
> Monsters of earth through earth we stray,
>   And how remission comes, God knows.

Nowhere in *Whipperginny* do there appear any signs that remission is possible. Ironic restraint and the recognition of dichotomy are the two chief lessons taught. When, as in "The Ridge Top," a note of triumph is struck, the poet's words sound premature and hollow. One poem in the book, however, "The Bowl and Rim," suggests that the opposites are not truly opposite, that thought is not a battle but a dialectic. The poem tells of a rabbi and a friar, who are chained to one another in the same cell for seven years, at the end of which each has grafted something of the other's thought upon his own, and both can say of Jesus in unison:

> *Man-like he lived, but God-like died,
>   All hatred from His thought removed,
> Imperfect until crucified,
>   In crucifixion well-beloved.

Thus the age-old war between Christianity and Judaism, the platter's bowl and its rim, is reconciled; the two religions are in fact one, just as in "The Song of Contrariety" distance itself is shown to be illusory:

> Far away is close at hand,
>   Close joined is far away.

Thus the way of escape appears to lie not through remission of sin but by the acceptance of paradox. The keyword to this phase of Graves's thought is, like Goethe's, "Restraint": the restraint shown by the two princes whose meeting is recorded by the Chamberlain.

Graves's acceptance, however, and his advocacy of restraint, seem sometimes to be accompanied by a half-shrug of the shoulders. The paradox and the unknowable do not arouse in him any feeling of awe, but rather, as often in Thomas Hardy, a suspicion that life may be a joke practised on us by an indifferent deity.

Between the appearance of *Whipperginny* and that of the *Collected Poems 1914–1926*, Graves published four small

books in more or less restricted editions. He had given
up his hopes of attracting a broad public. The response to
new poetry was at that time diminishing. The Georgians
had lost their brief popularity; the new poetry of Eliot,
Pound, and the Sitwells, so much more consciously
modern than Graves's, set a standard of modishness to
which many lesser poets attempted to conform. Graves,
though consistently experimenting, failed to catch the
popular attention. The last hundred pages of the *Collected
Poems*, nevertheless, which contain selections from these
small books together with a handful of pieces hitherto
uncollected, confirmed Graves's claim to be one of the
most distinguished English poets then writing.

Many of the new poems repeat the motifs of the old.
"Twin Souls" takes up the subject of "The Bowl and
Rim," and "The North Window" reverts to the upside-
down theme that occurred in "Outlaws," while at the same
time arousing an echo from the more distant "Boy in
Church." Here, however, the church or chapel is drawn
double. There is the building itself, opaque from within,
whose windows protect the worshippers from the sight
of the damned rising from their tombs in Stanley Spencer
realism on All Soul's Eve. But there is another chapel
moulded out of the stormy darkness by the light which
pours out through the chapel window, which is transparent from without. And the subject of the glass is *The
Hour of Doom*, in which the Saviour divides the sheep
from the goats, though the damned derive an entirely
contradictory lesson from the picture since they are looking
at it from the outside,

  *With the scene reversed, and the legend backwards too,
   Displaying in scarlet and gold the Creator who damns,
   Who has thrust on His Left the bleating sheep and the
     lambs,
   Who has fixed on His Right the goats and kids accursed,
   With *Omega : Alpha* restoring the last as first:

> Then the psalms to God that issue hence or thence
> Ring blasphemy each to the other's Omnipotence.

The poem has been dropped from the author's complete collection, perhaps because the intellectual or secondary implications are not fully worked out. The poem may allegorise the contradictions between conscious and unconscious mind, and their irreconcilability. It may speak of the unbearable stuffiness of that church in which the boy once had sat comfortably protected from the storm and the ghosts outside. Certainly Graves's thought was moving in the direction of agnosticism. One cannot think of "In the Wilderness" as more than a decorative poem with an unorthodox Christ as its central figure. Nothing in the early Graves speaks of religious feeling. Among the new pieces "Knowledge of God," "The Rainbow and the Sceptic," and "Essay in continuity" postulate an unknowable deity. In the first there is an echo of the Pythagorean belief in eternal recurrence, perhaps derived from conversations with an Indian philosopher who figures under an initial in the poem "To M. in India":

> *The caterpillar years-to-come
>   March head to tail with years-that-were
> Round and round the cosmic drum,
> To time and space they add their sum,
>   But how is Godhead there?
>
> Weep, sleep, be merry, vault the gate
>   Or down the evening furrow plod,
> Hate and at length withhold your hate,
> Rule, or be ruled by certain fate,
>   But cast no net for God.

The poem "Alice," the most accomplished of those in the section written between 1923 and 1926, leaves no loose ends, and is rather a plea for relativism of judgment than, like the last poems considered, a more or less jaunty statement of agnosticism. At this period Graves appears frequently to have been carried away by his facility with the ballad metre and similar measures into making loosely defiant statements that sometimes contain echoes from earlier poets. Either Housman or Henley may have contributed something to the last two verses quoted. The flat blank verse of the "Lord Chamberlain," or the unemphatic rhymed pentameters of the trivial story of deliberate international misunderstanding "Diplomatic Relations," is far better suited to the argument that he now wished to develop. It is significant that in the rhymed couplet also Graves is sometimes betrayed into facile thinking by a too plangently repetitive rhyme or accentual scheme. If "The North Window" fails, as the poet believes it does, some part of the blame must be attributed to the emphatic beat of the rhymes. The argument of "Alice" benefits from the off-hand nature of its rhyming, an accented syllable being sometimes matched with one that carries a very slight accent, a feminine rhyme sometimes alternating with a masculine. Graves's tendency to break down conventional measures, which began with his Skeltonics, and reached a peak of accomplishment in "Rocky Acres," is here unobtrusively continued. The relativism of the poem's thought is echoed in the irregular beat of the lines. Alice, "the prime heroine of our nation," in climbing through the Looking Glass into a palace of reversed significances—the poem is a fresh and more successful treatment of the "North Window" theme, written on a lower emotional level—accepts the paradoxes that she finds. "With proper British phlegm" she refuses to make the easy assumption that the two worlds must be made to correspond. Unworried by the contradiction between inside and outside, she set out

  *To learn the rules and moves and perfect them,

and thus with six moves only won her crown. The world

through the looking glass is a world where Victorian logic no longer prevails and poetry begins. For the first time Graves brings the creative act into the argument. Dream and nightmare now yield to poetry. The fears which had for so long haunted this other world for him are now dispelled, and its limits are recognised. If it does not impinge on everyday reality, everyday reality will not attempt to impugn its validity within its own territory: a visit to the other side will be "queer but true."

> *For Alice though a child could understand
>   That neither did this chance-discovered land
>   Make nohow or contrariwise the clean
>   Dull round of mid-Victorian routine,
>   Nor did Victoria's golden rule extend
>   Beyond the glass: it came to the dead end
>   Where formal logic also comes; thereafter
>   Begins that lubberland of dream and laughter,
>   The red and white flower spangled hedge, the grass
>   Where Apuleius pastured his Gold Ass,
>   Where young Gargantua made whole holiday;
>   But further from our heroine not to stray,
>   Let us observe with what uncommon sense,
>   Though a secure and easy reference
>   Between Red Queen and kitten could be found,
>   She made no false assumption on that ground
>   (A trap in which the scientist would fall)
>   That queens and kittens are identical.

The quotation follows the poem's original form. In the revision which stands in the 1959 *Collected Poems* some cuts are made in the argument, though not in this conclusion, which only differs—except in punctuation—from the original in the somewhat un-Carrollian substitution of "Where empty hearses turn about" for "Where formal logic also comes." This extension of the metaphor with its surrealist overtones breaks the Victorian illusion a little too brusquely; and the earlier omission of references to Einstein and Euclid perhaps overtautens the poem's already taut argument. The problem of rewriting is perhaps less acute here than in the previously analysed case of "The Pier Glass," where an attempted resolution of the poem is omitted and the poem left in the air.

The poem "Alice" is free from fear. The dispersion of fear is the subject of the unjustly rejected "From Our Ghostly Enemy," which tells of a haunted man who, on his wife's advice, confronts his ghost. The ghost then ceases to plague him:

> *She answered him, simple advice
>   But new, he thought, and true.
> 'Husband of this be sure,
> That whom you fear the most,
>   This ghost fears you.
>
> 'Speak to the ghost and tell him,
>   "Whoever you be,
> Ghost, my anguish equals yours,
> Let our cruelties therefore end.
>   Your friend let me be." '
>
> He spoke, and the ghost, who knew not
>   How he plagued that man,
> Ceased, and the lamp was lit again,
>   And the reign of peace began.

With this new freedom from fear a new and more kindly irony also entered in Graves's poetry, of which the best examples, "The Clipped Stater," a poem addressed to T. E. Shaw or Lawrence, and "Virgil the Sorcerer," have been the most undeserved of all the victims of Graves's poetic purges. The ironic manner of his poem afterwards became the stock-in-trade of the accomplished American classicist John Crowe Ransom, a selection from whose works Graves sponsored for English publications. Almost all Ransom's virtue can be traced to such a verse as that in which, in this poem, Graves introduces Alexander:

> *He would not take a Goddess to his Throne
> In the elder style, remembering those disasters
> That Juno's jealous eye brought on her Consort.
> Thaïs was fair; but he must hold his own.

Ransom's irony is at times a little facile; Graves uses it however for more serious effects. The poem to Lawrence tells of an Alexander who survives his supposed death and, flown off with by a djinn, enlists as a frontier guard on the borders of China. Here he is by chance paid with a stater that bears his own august head. The reference to the reincarnation of Lawrence of Arabia as Aircraftsman Shaw is obvious. Yet the poem is principally concerned with Graves's favourite theme of relativity. For at the conclusion, though the beaten soldier who was once emperor of half the world ponders as he recognises the stater "coined from the bullion taken at Arbela,"

> *...he cannot fathom what the event may mean.
> Was his lost Empire, then, not all-embracing?
> And how does the stater, though defaced, owe service
> To a God that is as if he had never been?

Graves records, "Lawrence laughed and laughed when I sent him the poem."

Gods are but relative in their power, which is of short duration; and poets survive perhaps for merits that were never theirs. "Virgil the Sorcerer" relates the two legends of Virgil, classical and medieval, that of the master-poet and that of the sorcerer of Toledo, to speak of poetry as a rare inspiration that cannot be subordinated to programmes and ambitions:

> *Vanity: for proud resolution droops.
>   We are not Virgils, but one night in twenty:
> When we should step our masts we trundle hoops:
>   Art is most rare though boasts of art are plenty.

Yet in this poem Graves makes his greatest claim for
poetry as a power that can release men from their chains.
Virgil the sorcerer, wrongfully imprisoned, engineers
a break-out among his filthy fellow-captives, using the
magic of his art to draw a ship with charcoal upon the
walls, in which, by the powers of his imagination, they
will escape:

> *'Who will not launch with me on midnight air
>   A ship of hope, through the cold clouds to skim?'
> They gazed at Virgil in a quick despair
>   Knowing him mad; yet gently humoured him,
>
> Quietly watched while on the prison wall
>   He scratched a galley, buoyant and well-found.
> 'Bring sticks for oars.' They brought them at his call.
>   'Up then and row!' They stepped from solid ground.

But the poem ends on a divided note in which pessimism
prevails.

> *What Virgil did can yet again be done.
>   Poetry is a spell of furious power,

Graves proclaims, yet protests in conclusion that "Time
the limiter wears us to rags," till

> *   we condone
> The unmoving present: on a mound of mud
> We loll red-eyed and wan, whittling a bone,
>   Vermined, the low gaol-fever in our blood.

Here for the first time Graves condemns his age as one of
decadence; the theme is many times repeated in some of
his best poems of the Thirties. For when the slump came
and Fascism arose Graves, though immediately after the
war a Labour Party supporter, did not see the crisis as
soluble on political lines. Rather he saw it in a broad
conspectus of history as a repetition of disasters that had
struck previous Empires, Alexander's, the Roman, and

the Chinese. The poet is isolated and forgotten; once an Emperor,

> *He is enlisted for the frontier guard
> With gaol-rogues and the press-gang's easy captures;
> Where captains who have felt the Crown's displeasure,
> But have thought suicide too direct and hard,
>
> Teach him a new tongue, and the soldier's trade,
> To which the trade *he* taught has little likeness.

Lawrence's choice of an anonymous soldier's life, Graves's own war experience and the need to earn a living not by poetry but by miscellaneous writing or teaching, unite to make the Alexander of "The Clipped Stater" a figure representative of his condition. The Virgilian escape by the imagination was always possible. Yet to rely on it was vain, since, as I have just quoted, "We are not Virgils, but one night in twenty."

"The Marmosite's Miscellany," contributed to the *Calendar of Modern Letters* under the pseudonym "John Doyle," is a Skeltonic attack on the state of literature in 1925 put into the mouth of a learned monkey, interviewed in a World Exhibition. References to Apuleius, Skelton, and Samuel Butler in the past, and to the leading Georgian figures in the present, also three or four pages of notes, make the poem a somewhat private satire; there is no generality of application until the end, when Graves makes a clear declaration of poetry's failure to interest those "square-headed merchants of practical parts," the burghers of "Rocky Acres":

> *   We serve a lost cause: does any pride remain
>   In prolonging tradition beyond its due time,
>   Giving it lip-service, mumbling and vain,
>   With a measured metre and expected rhyme?
>   Morning and evening our ancient bells chime,
>   Yet the whole congregation could sit in one pew,
>   The sexton, the verger, and old folk one or two.

"The Marmosite's Miscellany" gave Graves, as he felt, one last chance of "roaring" before the church of poetry was disestablished, of attacking the philistines and of exposing his more fashionable contemporaries, whose practice was to take

> *A sniff at every flask
> And a lick at every stopper.

The accomplishment of the poem's early verses, whose subjects are restricted by deliberate mock-medieval convention to subjects beginning with the letter M, is the equal of Skelton's, and Graves's chance-bred mythology also—

> *Mnevis in the likeness of a Golden Calf
> Disputing for power with Jehovah the Just

—looks forward to future and more serious incursions into this field. If the poem remains a *jeu d'esprit*, it is because Graves's playful and rumbustious anger is backed by little thought.

The final poems of the 1914–1926 volume speak of the problem of communication between lovers and perhaps also between poet and reader. In "Pure Death" and "The Cool Web," Graves speaks of an attempt so completely to break down isolation that two people may even exchange deaths. When "giving presents became a malady," the lovers in "Pure Death" attempted to give the ungivable, the pride of the private and isolated self, and mutually to acknowledge their terror in the face of death. This is shown as the supreme gift; and a miracle equal to Virgil's occurs at the moment when

> Each with shaking hand unlocks
> The sinister, long, brass-bound coffin-box,
> Unwraps pure Death, with such bewilderment
> As greeted our love's first acknowledgement.

In "The Cool Web," on the other hand, this ultimate

facing of truth is seen to be disastrous. There is, the poet
says, a final truth from which we are protected by the
"cool web" of language, which also protects us from that
immediacy of experience that we have known in childhood. "If we let our tongues lose self-possession," he
concludes,

> Before our death instead of when death comes,
> Facing the wide glare of the children's day,
> Facing the rose, the dark sky and the drums,
> We shall go mad no doubt and die that way.

Like King George's dumplings in "Dumplings' Address
to Gourmets," we must be content with our dumpling-
hood, and refrain as men from discussing what ceases to
be real as soon as it is discussed.

Approaching the borders of the incommunicable,
Graves did not press on like the Eliot of the *Quartets* but,
eschewing private statements, henceforth extended his
powers of inventing and elaborating myths, thus turning
away from a new temptation towards Romanticism to
entrench himself in a Classical stoicism. Advancing far
beyond the self-conscious myth-making of "The Bedpost,"
Graves reached the position of the symbolists, whose
myths were born with their poems and were from the
first inseparable from them.

REFERENCES

1. *G.B.*, pp. 238–64.
2. *G.B.*, pp. 239–40.
3. *G.B.*, p. 246.

4. *G.B.*, pp. 261–2.
5. *G.B.*, p. 262.

CHAPTER III

CHECKMATE

Robert Graves's interest in contemporary American poetry, beginning with his advocacy of John Crowe Ransom, E. E. Cummings, and others in his essay on *Modernist Poetry*,[1] continued in the form of a literary alliance, offensive and defensive, with the poet Laura Riding, who began to exercise a great influence on his work and opinions. The prevailing mood of his collection *Poems 1926–30* was the sentimental-ironic, a peculiarly American state of mind expressed by Graves's follower Crowe Ransom, but far more aggressively by Cummings, Marianne Moore, and William Carlos Williams. The sophisticated and allusive idiom of these poets, with its apparently off-hand cleverness, was no doubt the product of the American writer's isolation from any broad public, a situation far worse than that of his English colleagues. The same isolation, perhaps even intensified, explains the academic obscurity of more recent American poets, many of whom are members of university teaching staffs.

Under the stress of private events hinted at the end of *Good bye to All That*,[2] and allusively referred to at somewhat greater length on the last pages of the first edition, Graves cut himself off from many of his friends, retiring into a private fortress.

The danger that, when written in the distrustful attitude which Graves now adopted, poetry might degenerate into a private activity pursued without an audience was countered at this stage by an attack on the neglectful reader. Just as Edith Sitwell baited the

audiences that came to her recitals and embarked on
controversies in the press, so Laura Riding in the preface
to her *Collected Poems* starts a brusque offensive against
the ignorant and careless reader:

Because I am perfectly aware of the background of
miseducation from which most readers come to poems,
I begin every poem on the most elementary plane of
understanding and proceed to the plane of poetic
discovery (or uncovering) by steps which deflect the
reader from false associations, false reasons for reading.
No readers except those who insist on going to poems
for the wrong reasons should find my poems difficult;
no reader who goes to poetry for the right reasons
should find them anything but lucid; and with few
other poets are readers so safe from being seduced into
emotions or states of mind which are not poetic.

Thus the complete onus is thrown on the reader, who
if he fails to appreciate the poems merely reveals his own
miseducation or defective motives. The poems are indeed
in many cases lucid. Their weakness lies in their resolute
exclusion of emotions or states of mind which are, by
Laura Riding's peculiar definition, unpoetic. The effect
of this puritanical theory on the poet of "The Presence"
and "Virgil the Sorcerer" was rapid and radical. The
conversational vagaries of her poetry can be exemplified
by the opening lines of "Death as Death":

> To conceive death as death
> Is difficulty come by easily,
> A blankness fallen among
> Images of understanding,
> Death like a quick cold hand
> On the hot slow head of a suicide.
> So is it come by easily
> For one instant . . .

Compared with Graves's almost contemporary:

> This I admit, Death is terrible to me,
> To no man more so, naturally,
> And I have disenthralled my natural terror
> Of every comfortable philosopher
> Or tall dark doctor of divinity:
> Death stands again in his true rank and order,

Laura Riding's analysis is coldly theoretical. Even when later she speaks of pain as something experienced, she starts with a negative statement:

> Pain is impossible to describe
> Pain is the impossibility of describing

and ends in accomplished word-play that echoes Gertrude Stein:

> Not mystery but pain not plain but pain
> But pain beyond but here beyond.

The poems of the 1926–30 collection, the majority of which had previously appeared in limited editions, bear the mark of Laura Riding's influence. Their general tendency is to turn away from feeling, and accept the "dumplings' " or purely human position to the neglect of all emotional or spiritual overtones. Many of them are no more than elaborate intellectual jokes, the forerunners of the "satires or grotesques" which Graves was later to write "for wits."

Laura Riding had, like Graves, amused herself by inventing sub-human monsters, the modish equivalent of fairies. Her Tillaquils were of this species, of whom she tells:

> Once only two Tillaquils nearly a man and a woman
> Violated a hopeless code with hope,
> Slept a single dream seeming in time.
> 'Come,' he cried, coaxing her,

'Stairs stream upward not for rest at every step
But to reach the top always before Death.'
'Softly,' she whispered,
'Or two Tillaquils will wake.'

The creatures are, as she says in her first line, almost
human. But by their refusal to wake up, or by deliberately avoiding difficult emotions, they are left

> With only a lost memory
> Punishing this foolish pair
> That nearly lived and loved
> In one nightmare.

"The Tillaquils" is an off-beat satire against the insensi-
tive; Graves's monster in the poem "Railway Carriage"
—since somewhat altered and renamed "Welsh Incident"—is fantastic, anti-social and perhaps Skeltonic by
descent. The creature whose emergence from "the sea-
caves of Criccieth" on an Easter Tuesday, and whose
loud and inopportune belch (changed in the later version
to "a loud, respectable noise—like groaning to oneself
on Sunday morning") led to untold repercussions, no
doubt incarnates the poet as poltergeist, or as a survivor
of the primitive gods—both are recurrent images in
Graves's poetry—or, in the words of "Rocky Acres," a
poem which also has a Welsh background, as the

> Terror for fat burghers in far plains below.

But this latest Welsh poem is also in part a satire against
Welsh garrulousness and inconsequence, and is rhythmi-
cally conceived to be read in a Welsh sing-song. It is in
fact, like "Lift Boy," a poem that bears more obvious
traces of Laura Riding's influence, principally intended
as a fantasy

> *very neatly*
> *Contrived to make you and me*
> *Laugh.*

Fantasy and laughter enter largely into the 1926–30
volume, and with them a pessimism sometimes tempered
as in "Gardener" and sometimes in the pure concentration of "Ship Master." Graves can either say of man in the
person of his "Gardener".

> Well, he had something, though he called it nothing—
> An ass's wit, a hairy-belly shrewdness
> That would appraise the intentions of the angel
> By the very yard-stick of his own confusion,
> And bring the most to pass . . .

or in the person of his ship-master in the poem which he
afterwards renamed "The Furious Voyage," set out on
the uncharted journey of his life in a

> vessel, dead from truck to keel,
> With its unmanageable wheel,
> Its blank chart and the surly crew,
>
> In ballast only due to fetch
> The turning point of wretchedness
> On an uncoasted, featureless
> And barren ocean of blue stretch.

The vein of paradox, however, already explored in "The
Bowl and the Rim" and "North Window," now began
to reappear. It informs the not altogether successful
"Saint," which has been preserved, though with the loss
of its first three verses, in the 1959 collection. In it
Spenser's Red Cross Knight, after slaying his dragon,
turns hermit with the resurrected creature as his atten-
dant. The poem seems to carry secondary meanings
associated with Graves's former interest in psychoanalysis. For, in part at least, the Blatant Beast stands for
the Freudian "unconscious," and therefore, as the poem
suggests, is better left unslain since while he lives,

*The infamy of his ravage is delight.

This line disappears in the poem's final version, but the statement remains:

> Therefore no grave was deep enough to hold
> The Beast, who after days came thrusting out
> Wormy from rump to snout,
> His yellow cere-cloth patched with the grave's mould.

In the cancelled opening verses Graves gives as an additional reason why the Beast should be spared, the thought that the Knight, or conscious mind, has then always a "Laurel of salvation to look forward to," whereas once the Beast is dead it

> *   is carrion and a worse
> Than carrion.

Graves's refusal to countenance the destruction of evil is linked in this poem with his dislike of preachers, revivalists, and chapel-worthies, whom he had satirised in his Welsh poem "Railway Carriage," and who formed a good proportion of his victims in the opening section of "The Marmosite's Miscellany." In them he saw men whose seeming idealism is in fact a feebly disguised destructiveness, fed on the energy of their repressed vices. Therefore it is the Beast, even when "noisome with long decay" that triumphs in the end, mocking and discrediting his worthy slayer, whom he never forsakes even in death.

Graves applies a similar thought to his poetic and perhaps his physical ancestors in "Front Door Soliloquy," in which he proclaims that those "connected with all reigning houses" have the right to preserve their vices. For even though such a man may be no more than "grandeur's grandson," yet, speaking of him in the first person, Graves claims for him the right to

> dung on my grandfather's doorstep,
> Which is a reasonable and loving due
> To hold no taint of spite or vassalage
> And understood only by him and me.

The poet is free to react against the great poetic tradition. Yet the lackeys of the house must promptly drive off the burgherly unpoetic, the

> bog-rat-whiskered, mean, psalm-griddling
> Lame, rotten-livered, which and what canaille

since

> This house is jealous of its nastiness.

At this point, by proclaiming himself "no Rousseauist, nor artists of the world unite" Graves would seem to have moved politically to the right. Henceforward he is a defender of the old culture rather than an advocate of the new.

But the most persistent note in this poetry written between Graves's thirty-first and thirty-fifth years is not its lightness and fantasy, nor its greater or lesser pessimism, nor its exploitation of paradox, nor yet its continued campaigning against the self-satisfied, it is a new defeatism, an arguing away of experience. In "The Lord Chamberlain" he had rejected melodrama in favour of minimal gestures; in "The Dumplings' Address" he had advocated man's acceptance of his dumpling-hood, and in "Virgil the Sorcerer" he had counter-balanced great claims for the poet's magical powers by a final admission of his present-day impotence. But in such a poem as "The Castle," Graves effectively denies the possibility of any escape from the prison of one's own life or thoughts:

> There's no way out, no way out—
> Rope-ladders, baulks of timber, pulleys,
> A rocket whizzing over the walls and moat—
> Machines easy to improvise.
> No escape,
> No such thing: to dream of new dimensions,
> Cheating checkmate by painting the king's robe

> So that he slides like a queen;
> Or to cry, 'Nightmare, nightmare!'
> Like a corpse in the cholera-pit
> Under a load of corpses.

Physical love is rejected in "Sandhills" as leading only to multiplication

> *By two and two and two and two again,

and the reader too is flung off, as an old enemy that peers over the poet's shoulder, thrusting himself against him and confusing his thoughts, in "The Reader over My Shoulder," who is here drawn rather as an internal critic, or at least as one who echoes the poet's self-criticisms, than as that contemporary to whom Graves has, both before and since, endeavoured to give an ordered poetic account of himself. Again Graves's proclamation is over-strident:

> For you in strutting, you in sycophancy,
> Have played too long this other self of me,
>   Doubling the part of judge and patron
> With that of creaking grindstone to my wit.
> Know me, have done: I am a proud spirit
>   And you for ever clay. Have done.

This same reader is even more cruelly pilloried in the brief "Bay of Naples," his response to poetry itself being compared to that of

> *The blind man reading Dante upside-down
>   And not in Braille . . .

But most remarkable among the negations in Graves's poetry of this time is "The Terraced Valley," in which he once more denies all possibility of escape even as he describes an actual moment of escape from that confinement characterised in "The Castle," an escape into another dimension of experience more real than that which Alice reached when she climbed through the

looking glass, or than the world of the damned outside
the North Window, which was marked by a similar
reversal of left and right to that of this latter poem. The
moment actually described is mysterious since the experience is analysed almost before it is described:

> In a deep thought of you and concentration
> I came by hazard to a new region:
> The unnecessary sun was not there,
> The necessary earth lay without care—
> For more than sunshine warmed the skin
> Of the round world that was turned outside-in.

Was it a moment of mystical certainty, or mere disturbance of the consciousness, or an unheralded descent into
the lubberland of dream? Suddenly the features of the
landscape were seen in reversed relationship; and in the
second phase of the experience love itself was "herma-
phrodized." Sun and sky had disappeared, giving place
to their inner counterparts, and now love too had disappeared. The whole nature of things was transformed
into its opposite:

> Neat this-way-that-way and without mistake:
> On the right hand could slide the left glove.
> Neat over-under: the young snake
> Through an unyielding shell his path could break.
> Singing of kettles, like a singing brook,
> Made out-of-doors a fireside nook.

The poet had come to a region which bore the same
relation to the real as the world of the Red Queen to the
drawing-room of Alice's Victorian family, and fear for
the loss of his beloved summoned him back,

> I knew you near me in that strange region,
> So searched for you, in hope to see you stand
> On some near olive-terrace, in the heat,
> The left-hand glove drawn on your right hand,
> The empty snake's egg perfect at your feet.—

E   R.G.

But found you nowhere in the whole land,
And cried disconsolately until you spoke
Immediately at my elbow, and your voice broke
This trick of time, changing the world about
To once more inside-in and outside-out.

The last lines are quoted in a revised form in which the
epithets in particular are more precise and less loosely
evocative than those of the original version. The argument of the poem is tautened, but the nature of this
"trick of time"—the phrase comes only in the revised
version—is hardly dwelt on and its implications are not
explored at all. If it was as it seems a moment of escape
from time it was not essentially different from Eliot's
moment in the rose-garden in "Burnt Norton," from
which the whole of the *Four Quartets* sprang. But it was in
Graves's nature to reject such experience. Though his
argument is often cast in a metaphysical form, his attitudes have been consistantly anti-metaphysical. Perhaps
his early conditioning to psychoanalysis is the factor that
has most consistently caused him either to accept the
illogical and the paradoxical with a shrug, or to reduce
them to plain terms. The idea of God's immanence and
infinitude is used as an ironic text in "To be less Philosophical," the moral of which appears to be that it is
better not to think of such things. If God is *He*, *She*, *It*,
We, *You* and *They*, and all are interchangeable, then
Each will partake of all, and *We*, as the sanest voice in the
chorus, will clearly abandon all thought about the Nature
of God:

> * *We* are also gradually tending
> To be less philosophical,
> To speculate more confusedly
> And defy the universal.

One outstanding characteristic of Graves's poetry which
was strongest during this period of his partnership with

CHECKMATE 59

Laura Riding was his defiance of the universal. Each poem sets out a special case. If any generalisations can be made, they are of man's insignificance, which is the theme of the poem "Midway." This piece has, however, been greatly altered since its original appearance in the 1926–30 volume, an off-hand relativism being substituted for the equally off-hand statement in the original version that man "improvises God."

> Nothing that we do
> Concerns the infinities of either scale.
> Clocks tick with our consent to our time-tables,
> Trains run between our buffers. Time and Space
> Amuse us merely with their rough-house turn,
> Their hard head-on collision in the tunnel.

All feeling of mystery, in the Wordsworthian sense, which persisted as an ingredient in English poetry up to the time of the Georgians, is here expressly repudiated. There is for Graves no bridge between the natural and supernatural; the latter can only be described in terms of the former. There still remains for him, however, an escape into magic beyond the glass to which "Victoria's golden rule extends." The most exact ordnance survey will fail to plot the "Lost Acres," from which another poem in this collection derives its name. It is in this lost land, unplotted by any map, that the prehistoric gods persist, that the poet reigns in his double capacity of creator and destroying monster or scourge of the burghers. Of these "Lost Acres" he says:

> *Invisible, they have the spite
>   To swerve the tautest measuring-chain
> And the exact theodolite
>   Perched every side of them in vain.

To find them, all that we need is to go "In no Direction",

> *Nor to avoid the way
>   That was not avoided

> Directionless some other day
> Or that was avoided.

Always, except in "The Castle," there was for Graves
some remote possibility of escape. T. S. Eliot, in con-
sidering a railway journey, observes in "The Dry
Salvages":

> Fare forward, travellers, not escaping from the past
> Into different lives, or into any future;
> You are not the same people who left that station
> Or who will arrive at any terminus.

Here the accent is on the impermanence of the personality, and the final existence of nothing except the
present moment. Graves, by contrast, in "The Next
Time," considers the familiar journey "Between a first
hereafter and a second"—familiar, perhaps, because life
and experience are repeated—and concludes that the
compartment is not really locked. Next time the chances
may be different, and the poet may escape through some
cleft in the otherwise impassable texture of Space-Time:

> And when we passengers are given two hours,
>   The wheels failing once more at Somewhere-
>   Nowhere,
> To climb out, stretch our legs and pick wild flowers—
>   Suppose that this time I elect to stay there?

The question is unanswerable in philosophical terms.
But Graves has here rejected philosophy. In his rough-
house campaign against logic and its formal implications, he had, as we saw, written some extremely good
nonsense verse. His method, which developed from the
Skeltonic, now derives something from music-hall patter,
and something also from the deliberately zany repeti-
tions of Gertrude Stein. Nursery rhyme is occasionally
echoed, though without the early nursery sentimentality.
In "Warning to Children" the young are now treated as

premature adults, confronted with the necessity of coming to terms with the

> Endless world in which you say
> You live.

They are no longer considered too "dumb to say how hot the day is." They can on the contrary speak more strongly against "being philosophical" than any adult; it is the childish element in Graves, which had previously found a refuge in the land of nursery rhyme, that now sought to escape the harsh conclusions of logical thought by strumming such five-finger exercises as:

> *Guessing black or white,
>   Guessing white, guessing black.
> Guessing black or white,
>   Guessing white, guessing black.

Furthermore one of the most successful poems in the book is, by contrast with the childish inventions of *Country Sentiment*, founded on an actual memory of childhood. "Pavement," afterwards renamed "Wm. Brazier," presents a "Practical Chimney Sweep," in a robust and realistic portrait ironically pointed by the suggestion that if certain lines be suppressed, and certain memories glossed over, an entirely different and sweetened version of a harsh personality can be obtained. The last lines accept the cruder portrait and issue a rough defiance to genteel taste:

> Let them copy it out on a pink page of their albums,
> Carefully leaving out the bracketed lines.
> It's an old story—f's for s's—
> But good enough for them, the suckers.

Aggression plays a large part in the poetry of this volume. Even in such a fanciful and richly comic incident as that of "Return Fare," the account of an unprofitable visit to Ireland, there is a certain impatience with the characters encountered. A companion piece, "Single Fare," on the other hand, which tells of the return of the devils expelled from England to their native Scotland and Ireland, half identifies the Celtic kingdoms with the rumbustious spirit of poetry.

Two poems in Graves's next collection, *Poems 1930–1933*—"The Bards" and "Ogres and Pygmies"—portray the poet once more as a destroyer, redeveloping the theme adumbrated in "Rocky Acres," but then only marginal to the poem's meaning. In "The Bards" the treatment is simple, though in presenting the butts of his wilful primitives Graves seems to be making some side reference to the Yeats of the Byzantium poems. His relation to the poetry of his great predecessor has always been uneasy.

> It is a something fearful in the song
> Plagues them—an unknown grief that like a churl
> Goes commonplace in cowskin
> And bursts unheralded, crowing and coughing,
> An unpilled holly-club twirled in his hand,
> Into their many-shielded, samite-curtained,
> Jewel-bright hall where twelve kings sit at chess
> Over the white-bronze pieces and the gold.

The Bards themselves are simple figures marked with the plus sign of the poet's approval. Though they may falter and stumble, their grief is a true emotion, whereas the formal beauty of kings sitting at chess is a dead thing. The proof of this is given in the last lines, in which it is their grief or the power of their song, personified, that "leads off the queens"

> To stir his black pots and to bed on straw.

Graves's Ogres, on the other hand, though they present a heroic contrast to

> the sweet-cupid-lipped and tassel-yarded
> Delicate-stomached dwellers
> In Pygmy Alley,

are more violent destroyers than man or poet can accept.
The end of "Ogres and Pygmies," obscure and imperfect
in the first version, is hardly clarified in its later and less
enigmatic form:

> And who would judge between Ogres and Pygmies—
> The thundering text, the snivelling commentary—
> Reading between such covers he will marvel
> How his own members bloat and shrink again.

It is not clear whether the reader is despised for failing
to maintain the proportions of an ogre, or if something
between ogre and pygmy is accepted as man's natural
state. Certainly in the two or three poems with sexual
themes, "Ulysses," "The Succubus" and "Down,
Wanton, Down," the ogre's lust is contrasted unfavour-
ably with a new, unqualified positive sign, that of Love:

> Love may be blind, but Love at least
> Knows what is man and what mere beast;
> Or Beauty wayward, but requires
> More delicacy from her squires.

From this point personal love becomes a principal
theme in Graves's poetry. Indeed those of his poems into
which he introduces it are, today, his most successful. At
first Love is invoked only as the opposite of Lust, a theme
that he had hardly touched before the opening poems of
the 1930–33 volume. The poem "Ulysses" is the portrait
of a sexual adventurer to whom "Penelope and Circe
seemed as one." It is a protest against the persistence of
the appetites, and the domination of the flesh:

> One, two and many: flesh had made him blind,
>   Flesh had one pleasure only in the act,
> Flesh set one purpose only in the mind—
> Triumph of flesh and afterwards to find
>   Still those same terrors with which flesh was racked.

The only release from these terrors, as the poet states

in "Devilishly Disturbed," lies in action, whether the writing of a poem, the act of love, or even, as he suggests in the last verse, a glance of the eye or the utterance of speech:

> *Devilishly disturbed
>   By this unready mind,
> Its mouth so halting dumb,
>   Its eye so winking blind—
> Yet once the eye has seen
>   And once the mouth has said,
> The Devil awhile is numb,
>   My heel being on his head.

The nature of the Love with which the poet opposes this compulsion to see, to speak, and to act, if only to earn some momentary freedom from the devil of desire, is expressed in a kind of metaphysical aside, a flat childish patter reminiscent of Skelton and Gertrude Stein. It is chiefly in this language that Graves seems now to have been capable of making his limited affirmations:

> *To whom else less acquaint,
>   To whom else without taint
>   Of death, death-true?
>   With great astonishment
>   Thankfully I consent
>   To my estrangement
>   From me in you.

Graves's greater affirmations, such as the Yeatsian "On Portents," which has been admitted to the 1959 volume, and "The Fello'ed Year," which has been undeservedly suppressed, seem to accept that miracle which was denied in "The Terraced Valley." In the first a woman is drawn who shares with Yeats's Maud Gonne the capacity for disturbing history; in the second the poet prays for the cessation of time and the concentration of all the seasons in a single whole:

*   I the same, yet praying
That the twelve spokes of the round-fello'ed year
Be a fixed compass, not a turning wheel.

In the seven years covered by these last two collections, Graves's production of poetry had diminished, and his attention had turned, though with less conviction, to other forms of writing. At the same time the public response to poetry, which had been stimulated by the simplicities of the Georgians and the contemporary sentiment of the war poets, had fallen away. Robert Graves's name was in 1933 chiefly associated in the public mind with *Good-bye to All That*, which had been published at the moment when interest in the last war had revived and when the next still seemed very distant. As a poet, however, he received small notice. His reputation was eclipsed, as were those of the other poets of his generation, by the emergence in 1930 of W. H. Auden, Cecil Day Lewis, and Stephen Spender, whose poetry, which seemed at the time contemporary and political in a new way, began instantly to attract attention.

Graves accused Auden in his sixth Clark Lecture[3] of copying certain verbal tricks from Laura Riding. The parallels that he quotes suggest at first sight a considerable debt. But in fact the early Auden, whose "zinc-bright influence" Graves deplores, started as poet at a point where technique of this kind was in general fashion. Graves himself was deflected by it from his own true course. But Laura Riding was not the inventor of the calculated understatement and off-hand patter that characterised the various poems in Auden's first book which Graves criticised. The resemblances are caused rather by similarity of view-point than by plagiarism. Auden's taste in the poetry of the past and in that of his contemporaries was similar to that of Graves in this middle period, and of Laura Riding also. Indeed he appears to begin at the point that Graves had now reached. Such lines as these from "On Dwelling":

> Courtesies of good-morning and good-evening
> From rustic lips fail as the town encroaches,

strongly recall Auden's more detailed and critical view of
a derelict countryside in which the old values have de-
cayed, given in the opening lines of his Poem XI:[4]

> Who stands, the crux left of the watershed,
> On the wet road between the chafing grass
> Below him sees dismantled washing-floors,
> Snatches of tramline running to the wood,
> An industry already comatose,
> Yet sparsely living.

Auden's writing is more diffuse than Graves's. He is far
more prone also both to obscurity and to the pursuit of
the singular image. It is impossible to speak of direct
influence. All that can be said is that Auden resembles
Graves or Laura Riding principally in those passages
where he, like them, rejects an inherited romanticism and
turns playfully anti-philosophical in the manner of the
Thirties. Such lines as

> Voices explain
> Love's pleasure and love's pain
> Still tap the knee
> And cannot disagree
> Hushed for aggression
> Of full confession
> Likeness to likeness
> Of each old weakness . . .[5]

could well be by the Graves of "To Whom Else." The
attitude is the same. The psycho-analytical complexity of
the fifth and sixth lines is however proper to Auden alone,
for Graves's addiction to Freudian or Groddeckian theory
was not at this time so extreme that he would view a con-
fession as in fact an act of aggression against its recipient.

In general it may be said that had Graves's poetry been compared with Auden's at the moment of the latter's first impact, Auden would not have been credited with such great originality, nor would Graves's have been thrust back into the limbo of the near middle-aged.

From his home in Majorca, where he had migrated after the publication of *Good-bye to All That*, Graves took part in various controversies, adopting the role of the disgruntled exile, unappreciated in England but determined to present his private beliefs and prejudices on every occasion when the majority seemed to be marching out of step. He not only refused to allow his poems to appear in anthologies. He made a habit of printing miscellanies of prose and verse in Majorca and marketing them by subscription from there. He seemed to be trying to cut himself adrift from the literary world. In fact, however, his retirement not only led to a slow renewal of his poetic powers. It was also productive of a series of novels which captured him a very large audience.

REFERENCES

1. *C.A.*, pp. 61–167.
2. *G.B.*, p. 279.
3. *Cr. Pr.*, pp. 151–2.
4. W. H. Auden, *Poems*, London, Faber, 2nd ed. 1933, No. XI.
5. W. H. Auden, *Poems*, London, Faber, 2nd ed. 1933, No. X.

CHAPTER IV

AUTOBIOGRAPHY, HISTORICAL NOVELS, AND SOME POEMS

Good-bye to All That was published in 1929, at that point when public interest in the events of the war had suddenly revived. Remarque's *All Quiet on the Western Front* was the best-seller of the year. Among Graves's friends and fellow poets, Edmund Blunden had already had some success with his moving and personal memories of the fighting in France, *Undertones of War*, and Siegfried Sassoon was about to publish *Memoirs of an Infantry Officer*, the sequel to his *Memoirs of a Foxhunting Man*. In contrast to these last two books, which presented the war in some retrospect, Graves's autobiography was harshly actual, and its writing careless. Even in the revised edition of 1957, *Good-bye to All That* is not a shapely book; nor is its prose that of a poet. It is however remarkable for the clarity with which scenes, situations, and conversations of long ago are called to life. There seems to be no lapse of time between event and description, and there is no attempt on the writer's part to put the past into perspective. Graves explains the manner of the book's composition in his Prologue to the 1957 edition:

I partly wrote, partly dictated, this book twenty-eight years ago during a complicated domestic crisis, and with very little time for revision. It was my bitter leave-taking of England where I had recently broken a good many conventions; quarrelled with, or been disowned by most of my friends ... and ceased to care what anyone thought of me.

It is this last factor that gives the book its special

quality. It is the work of a man who is not trying to create an effect. Graves's experience of prose-writing was so far not great. Apart from his critical essays, he had written a popular life of his friend T. E. Lawrence, and two engaging and light-hearted contributions to the brilliant Today and Tomorrow Series, *Lars Porsena, or The Future of Swearing*, and *Mrs Fisher, or The Future of Humour*. In these not very important works he had, however, put into practice the advice given him long ago by a preparatory school master, and recorded in his autobiography,[1] to eliminate all phrases that could be done without, and to use verbs and nouns instead of adjectives and adverbs whenever possible. Graves, in fact, despite his Classical interests and influences, writes in a style that descends, like that of his contemporaries David Garnett and Rex Warner, rather from Bunyan and Defoe than from the more conscious stylists. This manner was particularly suitable to the direct and factual autobiography; it contributed even more, however, to the achievement of the Claudius novels and their successors, providing the leaven of modernity that made these historical reconstructions light and appetising.

Good-bye to All That is a tolerant book, that reveals in its author a reluctant sympathy with tradition even in its most fossilised state. His early descriptions of life at Charterhouse, while reinforcing the current criticisms of the pre-war public school system, is not a piece of special pleading. Graves came through with a considerable respect for the philistines among whom he had lived, and even for the absurd rituals and taboos to which all alike were subjected. He had a similar respect for the niceties of life in a battalion which still preserved some of the hide-bound customs of the peace-time army, instructing its officers and men in the minutiae of regimental history, even though as the war went on the ranks were almost entirely refilled after each disastrous battle with fresh drafts of conscripts from home.[2]

Graves's account of his boyhood is extremely objective. On such a subject as his early religious belief, expressed in the poem "In the Wilderness," and his subsequent lapse into agnosticism, he does not describe any emotional stress; and though in the revised edition he adds a little to his previously somewhat skimpy account of the difficulties arising from his partially German extraction— his mother was a von Ranke, a relative of the historian— the substance of his remarks[3] is no more than that it made him insist all the more indignantly on his being Irish, taking his self-protective stand on the technical point that solely the father's nationality counted. There is throughout the book no appeal for the reader's sympathy. Even such a statement as "At least one in three of my generation at school died . . . The average life expectancy of an infantry subaltern on the Western Front was, at some stages of the war, only about three months; by which time he had been either killed or wounded," is made dry-eyed.[4]

Graves's descriptions of climbing on Snowdon with George Mallory, who was afterwards lost on Everest, of his brief military training, and of trench life in France gain much from their accurate documentation. He seems to have taken as much care in collecting this material from his own early life as afterwards in collating the Roman historians for his Claudius books, or regimental records for those devoted to Sergeant Lamb. But even more is gained by his lifelike reconstruction of conversations. The welcome given to Graves on his first arrival in the trenches by Captain Dunn, a veteran who eventually proved to be two months younger than himself, recreates the whole rhythm of the man and his conversation in a manner that was later to prove most effective in the evocation of Graves's Roman figures:

Dunn did not let the war affect his morale at all. He greeted me very easily with: 'Well, what's the news from England? Oh, sorry, first I must introduce you.

This is Walker—clever chap from Cambridge, fancies himself as an athlete. This is Jenkins, one of these elder patriots who chucked up their jobs to come here. This is Price—joined us yesterday, but we liked him at once: he brought some damn good whisky with him. Well, how long is the war going to last, and who's winning? We don't know a thing out here . . .'[5]

Similar rhythms, though perhaps a little more formal, will be noticed in the conversations of Claudius and his Imperial relations.

The later chapters of *Good-bye to All That*, despite their telling sketches of T. E. Lawrence, Thomas Hardy, and other friends of Graves's post-war years, suffer from the fact that he is extremely reluctant to speak of private matters. Of his marriage, his children and their upbringing, his Oxford studies, his war neurosis, and the writing of his poems he tells us something. His brief stay in Egypt as Professor of English Literature at Cairo is the last event fully and amusingly recorded. The book leads up to a moment of unexplained crisis in the year of its writing, when Graves left England for Majorca. Among the things to which he here said good-bye was the habit of even guarded self-revelation. Unlike some of his contemporaries, he was henceforth unwilling to make his life the subject matter of his books. In describing the war, he could speak without revealing secrets. But post-war life was a private matter, and Graves had therefore to abandon autobiography.

Good-bye to All That introduced Graves's name to a vast new public that had never read his poetry. It revealed moreover certain qualities of the novelist in him. He had already written one or two melodramatic stories, of which one "The Shout," was subsequently published;[6] and had attempted a war novel some parts of which had been incorporated in his autobiography, but had been defeated by the necessity of introducing an artificial plot.[7] The

making of plots has never come easily to Graves. For-
tunately in his next venture, the two Claudius novels, history itself provided the framework. All that was necessary
was to fill in plausible events and characters, the hints for
which were already provided by the Roman historians.

Graves's attitude to the Classical past is that of one
bored by fourteen years of conventional linguistic training[8] who wished to make a fresh approach for himself and
was not afraid of iconoclasm. The decadence of the Roman
Empire fascinated him because of the parallel situation in
which he seemed to be living. The theme had been treated
in several of his poems; it was to be restated even more
determinedly in "The Fallen Tower of Siloam" and
"The Cuirassiers of the Frontier." Graves saw himself
somewhat as the Alexander of "The Clipped Stater," a
frontier guard on the border of a lost Empire, already
half-oblivious of the values for which it had once stood,
and certain to be overwhelmed by the next onrush of
barbarians. Similarly Claudius in his novel was the last
civilised man in a world of criminal intriguers. Though
he succeeded by guile in keeping himself alive, he was
none the less certain to be overwhelmed in the end.

I Claudius was published in May 1934, and went through
six editions before the end of the year. It was translated
into seventeen languages, and received two literary
prizes. The first of his series of historical novels, it ex-
ploited all the non-poetic talents of its author, while
stealing nothing from the poetry. This was a matter of
deliberate choice on Graves's part. Having decided that
poetry could not be made to pay for itself, and that if he
was not to take a teaching or journalistic post some
secondary form of production must be attempted,[9] he was
resolved to use his lesser talents as money-makers that
would leave him free to write the few poems that came
to him in as many drafts as they might require.

I Claudius is not in the modern sense a novel. It is a
careful reconstruction from all available sources of the

Rome of Augustus, Tiberius, and Claudius himself, and to this end Graves made use of all his interests: in the history and archaeology of the classical world, in military and political matters, and in the psychology of violence and crime. A novel is by definition concerned with character and motive; and the tendency since Henry James has been towards an ever greater emphasis on fluctuations in the consciousness of a few persons. *A la Recherche du temps perdu*, *Ulysses*, *To the Lighthouse* were the outstanding novels of the time. But just as in his poetry Graves largely ignored the experiments of the European avantgarde, making almost no use of the innovations which derived from Baudelaire and Rimbaud, so in his novels he refused to notice the examples of his contemporaries. Never in his writings had he shown any insight into character, and the people in *I Claudius* remain as flat as the portrait of Captain Dunn already referred to. Graves is interested in the tissue of events, in what follows from what, and in the solving of historical enigmas. This saves him from indulging in the long descriptions that make such novels as *Salâmbbo* dull reading. It saves him also from the artificial attempt to create atmosphere. Compared with the greatest writer of historical novels in English, Sir Walter Scott, Graves is a historical theorist before he is a novelist, and Scott primarily a novelist who chooses his subjects from the past because life seemed to him to have been more dramatic before the Napoleonic wars and the onset of industrialism. In the same way *I Promessi Sposi* is primarily concerned with character and adventure; its setting at the end of the sixteenth century is unimportant; it is merely chosen as a time when the psychological conflicts which interested Manzoni were most clearly exposed. Graves on the other hand is captivated by the past. He is not, however, concerned with the differences in psychology between one age and another. His characters, like Bernard Shaw's, are actuated by purely modern motives. In fact Graves is not

F   R.G.

greatly concerned with subtlety of motive or introspection. When the actions of his characters are explained it is usually by reference to thought and theory, never to illogical impulse. His attitude is that of the detective story writer; one master idea, be it poisoning by mushroom, or the prevalence of incest in the Imperial family, or, in the later novel *King Jesus*, Our Lord's actual descent from the Jewish royal house, is made to provide all the clues.

Graves's Roman world is in decay, stricken by the Punic Curse, of which the Sibyl of Cumae speaks to the deaf, lame, and stuttering Claudius in the first chapter of *I Claudius*. This, perhaps, sufficiently explains the unrelieved criminality of Livia, Agrippina, Tiberius, Caligula, and the rest of the royal house. With the exception of Claudius himself, and Germanicus, who has the virtues of a good military leader, only Claudius's shadowy mistress Calpurnia seems to possess any virtues. Graves has projected his new-found distrust of society and its motives to which he refers in the prologue to the revised edition of *Good-bye to All That* on to the ancient world that he called to life. But he brought several ingredients of his own age to his evocation of Imperial Rome. The young Claudius, wary and self-protective in the dangerous company of his elders, bears some resemblance to the young Graves among the philistines at Charterhouse. Again, as an amateur military leader with more reliable insights than the professionals, Robert Graves the infantry officer reappears as the Emperor Claudius conducting his campaign in Britain; and the greatest virtue that he attributes to Livy[10] in his novel is the very one that he has himself most persistently striven for: "He makes the people of Ancient Rome behave and talk as if they were alive now"; to which the ancient and carping Pollio replies in words that apply equally to Graves: "You credit the Romans of seven centuries ago with impossibly modern motives and habits and speeches. Yes, it's readable all right, but it's not history."

The Claudius novels are very readable comedies of evil, interspersed with often entertaining and sometimes learned digressions. While the characters' actions follow the events of their own day, in so far as they can be reconstructed from the historians, their speech, beliefs, and reasonings are those of witty and disillusioned modern persons. At their best they remind one of the early Aldous Huxley. But the conversation at the Empress Livia's dining table is closer to Noel Coward. Claudius begins by asking that great lady who is his grandmother why, despite his unattractive physical habits, she has on this occasion allowed him to dine with her:

She smiled: 'Well, I admit that your presence at table still causes me a certain amount of . . . But never mind. If I have broken one of my oldest rules that is my affair, not yours. Do you dislike me, Claudius? Be frank.'

'Probably as much as you dislike me, Grandmother.' (Could this be my own voice speaking?)

Caligula sniggered. Urgulania tittered. Livia laughed: 'Frank enough! By the way, have you noticed that monster there? He's been keeping unusually quiet during the meal.'

'Who, Grandmother?'

'That nephew of yours.'

'Is he a monster?'

'Don't pretend you don't know it. You *are* a monster, aren't you, Caligula?'

'Whatever you say, Great-grandmother,' Caligula said with downcast eyes.

'Well, Claudius, that monster there, your nephew— I'll tell you about him. *He's going to be the next Emperor!*'

I thought it was a joke. I said smilingly: 'If you tell me so, Grandmother, it is so. But what are his recommendations? He's the youngest of the family and though he has given evidence of great natural talent . . .'[11]

Claudius's last remarks provide a clue to Graves's attitude that has persisted even in his recent Penguin translations of Latin authors. "Recommendations" and "great natural talents" convey a double irony: that of Claudius who can see only negative qualities in his seemingly demure nephew, and the irony of the twentieth-century writer displaying by the use of strikingly modern language his disrespect for the monuments of the ancient world as erected for him by his schoolmasters. Graves at moments amuses himself by crowning the bust of Caesar with the steel helmet of a later Gallic War.

The Claudius novels owe much of their success to the Graves's irreverence. But they benefit also by the compensating virtue, that he explains the past in terms of present-day knowledge or plausible theory. Sometimes, however, theory tips over into implausibility. Claudius's campaign for the conquest of Britain is brilliantly and imaginatively described. The Britons are entrenched on Brentwood Hill, with one flank protected by a marsh, the other by a thicket. Claudius, without military experience, is anxious to avoid a frontal attack, and the eunuch Posides, entrusted with the turning of the marsh flank, works out a ruse that is both anachronistic and incredible:

Posides answered: 'You have given me the easier flank, Caesar. There is, as it happens, a track through the marshes. One would have to go along it in single file, but there is a track. I met a man in London yesterday, a travelling Spanish oculist who goes about the country curing the people of marsh-opthalmia. He's in the Camp now, and he says he knows that marsh well, and the track—which he always uses to avoid the toll-gate on the hill. Since Cymbeline's death they have been levying no fixed toll, but a traveller must pay according to the amount of money he has in his saddle-bags, and the oculist got tired of being skinned.'[12]

The use of London for Londinium and the introduction of an occasional word of modern German into the mouth of a soldier from beyond the Rhine are no doubt legitimate devices. But it is doubtful whether any person in the first century would describe a disease in any terms that could reasonably be translated "marsh-opthalmia," or would describe himself as an "oculist." Nor is a toll-gate on an ancient British track very easy to believe in.

The Claudius novels continue and develop in an original way a tendency in the movement of historical fiction of which Lion Feuchtwanger with his *Ugly Duchess* (*Die hässliche Herzogin*, 1923: transl. 1927) and *Jew Süss* (*Jud Süss*, 1925: transl. 1926) was so far the leading practitioner. But whereas Feuchtwanger's originality lay in the application of modern psychological analysis to characters in the past, Graves achieves a similar effect by the mere use of modern language. "Advisory assistant to the Chief Vestal in moral matters"; "to avoid the scandal Livia paid up"; "a dreadful old woman with a cleft chin and hair kept black with lamp-soot (the grey showing plainly at the roots)": all these touches taken from a single page[13] cumulatively build up the impression that the Romans of the Empire were no more than twentieth-century people in period costume. Whereas the tradition of the novel from Sir Walter Scott and Alexandre Dumas to the many minor practitioners of the generation of Conan Doyle and Stanley Weyman had been to present the characters of the past as more admirable and heroic or more villainous than those of the present, the new historical novel stressed rather the unchangingness of human motive and action.

In *Count Belisarius*, Graves's next important novel of 1938, he retreated from the extreme position to which he had advanced in the Claudius books. Here the historical and military interest is subordinated to the personal drama, yet even the Belisarius—Antonina—Theodosius love-triangle, the central intrigue of the book, follows the narrative of Procopius. Graves claims that only one character in this teeming book is of his own invention. For the rest hints at least were provided by the sixth-century Byzantine historian in his *Secret History* (Historia Arcana), in which he attacked the Emperor Justinian and his Empress Theodora, or in his account of Justinian's campaigns and of his building activities. Graves had in fact as much material to draw on for this little-known period of Byzantine history as he had had for the better-known Claudian epoch. Here, however, his concern with military campaigns, his detached interest in religious heresies, his power of presenting the clashes of people and factions, combine to make this essay in fictionalised history as dramatic, though rather more slow-moving, than his two previous exercises in historical fiction. It is also better constructed. For whereas the excursus on the Druids in *Claudius the God*[14] is clearly a digression, the various accounts of military training and organisation in *Count Belisarius* form an intrinsic part of the story. Belisarius is, like Claudius, "the one good man in a wholly bad world." He is indeed described in these words in the horoscope that is cast for his future wife Antonina.[15] The Emperor Justinian, by contrast, is characterised, in the horoscope of his Empress-to-be, Theodora, then a cheap actress and prostitute, as "the King of the Demons." For the world of Belisarius is, as Graves sees it, like that of Claudius, in decay, the prey to Goths, Huns, Vandals, Moors, and Gepids, and to the inner corruption of the Byzantine capital with its faction feuds, which affected even the most stalwart barbarians who fought it or took service with it. But Belisarius, the cavalry commander who preserved his loyalty to Justinian even though ill-treated by him, redeems the book, which does not present the picture of unrelieved evil of its predecessors. Belisarius, in fact, seems to offer a Christian forgiveness to his royal master, for in the last words given by Graves to the scribe whom he credits with the writing of his story, "Belisarius pitied Justinian for wishing to be a

Christian and yet wanting the knowledge of how to set about it."[16]

The style of *Count Belisarius* is more sober than that of the Claudius novels. Except in certain comic passages, like that in which the Empress makes fun of the old senator Hippobates, who had scorned her in her humble days,[17] there is little of the levity either of description or conversation that Graves allowed himself in the Claudius novels. The conversation too is less modish than that round the Empress Livia's table, and the anachronisms far less blatant than in the description of the battle of Brentwood Hill.

The two books about the American Revolution which follow, *Sergeant Lamb of the Ninth* and *Proceed, Sergeant Lamb*, apply the same process of research and reconstruction to a soldier of whom Graves had first heard when instructing his men in 1915 in the history of their regiment. This same Lamb, once of the Ninth, later became a sergeant in the 23rd regiment of the line, or Royal Welch Fusiliers. Here again no major characters were invented, and no opinions expressed that were not current at the time. Graves took advantage of a brief visit to America to sketch in his background, and adopted a style with slight eighteenth-century echoes to suit the tongue of his fictitious narrator, who was the Sergeant himself. Again, as in his classical novels, Graves has taken great pains to ensure the accuracy of his historical detail. On the subject of scalping, for instance, he is most circumstantial[18] while the campaigns are meticulously recorded, and the habits of Indians, French, New Englanders, Rebels, and Loyalists carefully distinguished.

The last of this series of historical novels, *Wife to Mr Milton*,[19] tells in the first person the tale of the sixteen-year-old girl who married the then thirty-three-year-old poet. It constructs, with care equal to that of any of the previous books, a picture of England in the sixteen-forties. It was an age that contained many features which attracted Graves: a plethora of religious cranks and creeds and of historical controversies, and a considerable campaigning interest. The setting of the book also was in that Oxfordshire country which he knew so well. Graves was, however, deflected into the writing of a type of pastiche that now brought him far closer to the conventional writer of historical fiction. The conversation of his characters is stiff; the narrative follows seventeenth-century rhythms, and uses the vocabulary of the time. Graves's attitude in this novel is more ambivalent than that in the Claudius books or in *Count Belisarius*. At bottom, he does not care much for Milton or for his age. Though willing to ape his language and expound his thought, he comes rather to mock than to worship.

The last three novels were all written in England during the years of the Second World War. Graves had, however, been forced to return home before the outbreak of hostilities at the opening of the Civil War in Spain, which made his continued residence in Majorca impossible. Unlike the poets of the succeeding generation he expressed no judgments on the Spanish issue. Only from the sketch "Está en su casa"[20] does it appear that his sympathies were, on balance, with the Republican side.

In the twelve years between *Poems 1930–33* and the conclusion of the war, after which he was able to return to his house in Majorca, Graves despite the bulk of his prose production wrote a number of poems, some of which were included in his second collected volume of 1938, but the majority of which had to wait for winnowing and inclusion until the publication of its successor of 1947.

The 1938 volume presented a new and somewhat puritanical portrait of its author, for many poems were dropped and few new ones added. Those which appeared here for the first time, however, continued in the line of the old, and were unaffected by the successful prose writing of this middle period.

Preoccupation with war, a leading theme in the novels, now reappears in the poetry, primarily as a result no doubt of the more threatening state of Europe and the fear of a second war against the Germans. Outstanding among these new war poems are "Recalling War," and "Defeat of the Rebels." Both attempt to see war in a new way, to view it as an inevitability, like the weather:

> What, then, was war? No mere discord of flags
> But an infection of the common sky
> That sagged ominously upon the earth
> Even when the season was the airiest May.

In this time "when death was young again," men greeted the new "duty to run mad" with mingled fear and delight; old importances came swimming back. Graves now, twenty years after his own participation in a campaign that had begun to assume for him "the nature look of time," made for himself an anatomy of war itself. The poem contains what appear to be wilful, perhaps parodistic, echoes of Rupert Brooke ("Never was such antiqueness of romance") in the lines which recall the emotional release of war, and of Wilfred Owen ("In ache of wounds beyond all surgeoning") at the end of the same verse; and the poem itself ends on the despairing note of inevitable recurrence:

> Down in a row the brave tin-soldiers fall:
> A sight to be recalled in elder days
> When learnedly the future we devote
> To yet more boastful visions of despair.

"Defeat of the Rebels," on the other hand, recalls no specific war, but takes the blame for the crimes of the defeated enemy on behalf of the victors. After the enemy's overthrow the loyal forces realise that they "never had been robbed" but for their "sloth and hesitancy." There is possibly some allusion here to the international situation of the time, for it was only thanks to

the sloth and hesitancy of the Western powers that Hitler
was permitted to arm. But it is seldom safe to read any
reference to actual events into Graves's poetry. The situation described is more probably a psychological one.

The second theme which had arisen long ago from
Graves's experience of the 1914–18 war, that of ghosts
and survival, continues to be treated in the poems written
between 1933 and 1938. Survival at last seems to be
established. In the poem "No More Ghosts," which
Graves took as the title-piece of a cheap selection from his
work made in 1940, he seemed to welcome a new freedom
from haunting:

> We are restored to simple days, are free
> From cramps of dark necessity,
> And one another recognize
> By an immediate love that signals at our eyes.

> No new ghosts can appear. Their poor cause
> Was that time freezes, and time thaws;
> But here only such loves can last
> As do not ride upon the weathers of the past.

The contrast between simple thought and sights, and
complicated or especial experience is the theme of a
group of love poems to which "The Ages of Oath," "End
of Play," and "The Climate of Thought" also belong.
Here the poet's conception of love has advanced beyond
the point at which it was contrasted with lust. Love has
become for him the one positive symbol of which he is
certain; the other, that of magic, which he was afterwards to treat in the poetry that sprang from *The White
Goddess*, is now hardly stressed. At this point in Graves's
poetic evolution Love, simplicity, and freedom have become almost equivalents, all bearing the plus sign. Even
those poems that speak of the end of an age, "The Fallen
Tower of Siloam" and "A Country Mansion," carry at
the same time a cryptic and secondary message of hope.

The final disaster is seen to bring relief; the collapse of
tradition implies the promise of a new life. There is a
strong parallel here with some of the later poems of
Edwin Muir, in particular "The Horses," with its vision
of a new civilisation in closer unison with nature after
the breakdown of a final war.

In Graves's "A Country Mansion" the ancient house
represents the inherited techniques of civilisation, and
more particularly of poetry, which the poet must forsake
for the "far roads" of experiment:

> This rebel does not hate the house,
> Nor its dusty joys impugn:
> No place less reverend could provoke
> So proud an absence from it.

> He has that new malaise of time:
> Gratitude choking with vexation
> That he should opulently inherit
> The goods and tithes of the extinct.

As ever, the prevailing note is of ambivalence. The poet
does not rebel against tradition, but feels unworthy of his
inheritance. He is driven therefore by the malaise of his
time to renounce what he cannot accept with an easy
conscience. It is clear however that Graves does not think
of tradition as dead. The house is alive although deserted.
For the sap is still

> brisk in the oak
> Of the great beams: if ever they use a saw
> It will stain, as cutting a branch from a green tree.

The Biblical tower of Siloam also brought freedom with
its fall. The disaster was not as fearful as the anticipation:

> already the collapse
> Powdered the air with chalk, and shrieking
> Of old men crushed under the fallen beams

> Dwindled to comic yelps. How unterrible
> When the event outran the alarm
> And suddenly we were free.

Compared with such earlier prophecies of collapse as
"Act V, Scene 5," and "The Cuirassiers of the Frontier,"
this new poem is sardonically optimistic. The only affir-
mation which the last-mentioned poem, the imagery of
which is closely connected with the novel *Count Belisarius*,
seems capable of offering is the one already hinted at in
"The Clipped Stater," that the mercenaries on the frontier are now the best custodians of civilisation:

> In Peter's Church there is no faith nor truth,
> Nor justice anywhere in palace or court.
> That we continue watchful on the rampart
> Concerns no priest. A gaping silken dragon,
> Puffed by the wind, suffices us for God.
> We, not the City, are the Empire's soul:
> A rotten tree lives only in its rind.

In these two pieces the poet prophesies; in "The Fallen
Tower of Siloam" he renounces the Cassandra role:

> It behoved us, indeed as poets
> To be silent in Siloam, to foretell
> No visible calamity.

The love poems added to the 1938 volume carry the
optimistic argument still further, reintroducing in concealed form autobiographical elements which the poet
had for long foresworn. "The Ages of Oath," for instance,
while speaking in the first place of a resolve to approach
love more simply, narrates in highly compressed form the
history of the poet's attitudes not only to his feelings but
to the writing of his poetry also. Beginning with an early
attraction towards "The lost, the freakish, the unspelt,"
which can be related to the psychologically complicated
Pier Glass poems and the metaphysical exercises of
"Alice" and "The Lord Chamberlain," he confesses later

to have become a virtuoso—this may refer to the Laura Riding period—and wonders whether he has not remained a virtuoso even though wishing to turn to

> simple sights, when tiring
> Of unicorn and upas.

Perhaps this simplicity continued to elude him. But he resolves, at the poem's conclusion, to make a new beginning:

> with oaths
> On the true book, in the true name,
> Now stammering out my praise of you,
> Like a boy owning his first love.

The poem ends on a question-mark. Has he indeed failed to reach this point hitherto? Certainly in this poem he wins through to a direct emotional statement that has been absent from his poetry for a long time. He reaches the same directness, though perhaps not the same simplicity, in another piece of this time, "End of Play," which speaks of the necessity for new and more scrupulous statement:

> We tell no lies now, at last cannot be
> The rogues we were—so evilly linked in a sense
> With what we scrutinized that lion or tiger
> Could leap from every copse, strike and devour us.

The subtle discovery in these lines that thought takes the colour of the object it dwells on provides a retrospective comment on the poems of the psychoanalytical period, when the "lion or tiger" of neurosis would jump out of the simplest thing scrutinised and the poetry at times seemed deliberately to encourage its ghosts. Now a stricter "Climate of Thought" was demanded in the poem of that name, a thought whose every element was justly balanced. It could be likened to a country in which there were

> Few birds, sufficient for such caterpillars
> As are not fated to turn butterflies;
> Few butterflies, sufficient for such flowers
> As are the luxury of a full orchard.

This country of thought is perhaps related to that land of reversed values, accepted in "Alice" and rejected in "The Terraced Valley." It has however a sobriety of outline that is not present in Alice's "lubberland of dream and laughter . . . where young Gargantua made whole holiday" nor yet in that in which left and right were reversed. Graves had now abandoned his metaphysical attitude; his positive signs in these poems of the immediate pre-war years are reserved for moments of emotional discovery alone. These moments have been recorded before, though with less belief in their permanence. In *Poems 1926–1930* the poem "Sick Love," quoted in the first chapter of this book, pleads for the acceptance of love even though it can only be short-lived:

> Take your delight in momentariness,
> Walk between dark and dark—a shining space
> With the grave's narrowness, though not its peace,

and the later "Never Such Love" pleads that the word itself shall never be spoken or written down, since to speak it is to "Blab idly the heart's fated inconstancy." The later love poems, however, are more confident.

The year 1942 saw Robert Graves for the first time in the position against which he and Laura Riding had cautioned all poets in their hard-hitting essays on Modernist Poetry, now reprinted in *The Common Asphodel*.[21] He appeared for the first time as the head of a school. Hitherto not only had he been without followers, but his work had not for many years received the attention that was its due. It had certainly been greeted with far less interest than the new poetry of the Thirties. Only one poet among the new arrivals, William Empson, seemed

to have learnt anything from him. Empson's compressed
intellectuality, however, made far fewer concessions to
the potential reader than Graves had done. In this third
year of the war there appeared a small volume in which
a group of new poems by Graves appeared side-by-side
with those of two younger men who could be accounted
his disciples. *Work in Hand* is introduced as a collection of
three small books under a single cover published in this
form "for economy and friendship." There is no actual
suggestion of school or discipleship. Yet the poems of
Alan Hodge, a friend and occasional poet, and of Norman Cameron, who continued to write poetry until his
premature death some ten years later, are for the most
part written to a prescription copied from the master.
Such a piece as Cameron's "The Wanton's Death" tells
in Graves's own manner a story which appears in the
first place to narrate a personal anecdote symbolically. A
woman demands of two men that they deny their own
natures and become their opposites, that the merman
take to the land and the landman to the sea. When both
refused this "test of transmutation," and each

> found a specious refuge,
> Merman a pool, landman a reefy foothold
> Both claiming still the guerdon of achievement,

she "mocked their lie." Yet it was not their relics but
hers that in the end rotted

> on the sea-wasted foreshore,
> Half-wooed, half-spurned by the land-tainted spindrift.

Cameron's poem appears to possess only this single
level of significance. A comparable poem by Graves in
the same collection, "Frightened Man," carries a secondary meaning, hinted at only but none the less present.
Indeed the poem cannot be understood without it. The
first twelve lines describe a sort of man, characterised in
the poem's original form as "feline," who is mysterious

to the poet and alien from him. The eight lines of the
second part appear to continue the description:

> They are punctilious as implacable,
> Most neighbourly to those who love them least.
> A shout will scare them. When they spring, they seize.
> The worst is when they hide from us and change
> To something altogether other:
> We meet them at the door, as who returns
> After a one-hour-seeming century
> To a house not his own.

The frightened men, from being objective portraits, suddenly dissolve, and become, by suggestion, lost elements
of ourselves. They have been away for a long time, yet
when they return to the house that is no longer theirs they
do not seem to have been absent for more than an hour.
We disown them, yet they are our own shadow-person-
alities.

Many of Graves's poems carry a secondary meaning as
imprecise as this, but as essential for any real understanding. "A Love Story," the first piece in Graves's part
of the 1942 book, appears to carry no more than a single
significance. Yet this shifts as the poem progresses. At
first we are given a highly dramatic winter landscape in
moonlight, which apes the colours of summer and arouses
horror in the poet. He is reminded of a similar scene in
his youth, which remained in his mind. Then he had

> fetched the moon home,
> With owls and snow, to nurse in my head
> Throughout the trials of a new Spring,
> Famine unassuaged.

The landscape is now internalised. Winter symbolises
the poet's inability to love; the moon is the image of a
woman; the new spring in which famine is unassuaged is
perhaps a love affair that did not move the poet's heart.
For in the third verse he acknowledges that the change of

season was "all lies," that owls were not truly transformed into nightingales. Moreover the moon's or
woman's image "turned beldamish." He is compelled
therefore in his concluding verse to restore his winter
scene and accept his own powerlessness to force events.
For the famine in him has merely evoked a "Queen
Famine" outside; emptiness has been matched with
emptiness:

> Dangerous it had been with love-notes
> To serenade Queen Famine.
> In tears I recomposed the former scene,
> Let the snow lie, watched the moon rise, suffered the
>   owls,
> Paid homage to them of unevent.

Here is sufficient primary meaning, and the poem perhaps contains no more. Yet the close identification of love
and poetry in "Mid-Winter Waking," which speaks of
the same struggle between spring and winter in the poet,
places poetry and a loved person ever more clearly together on the side of that season which wakes the poet
from his "long hibernation." The poem is in some sort a
sequel to "A Love Story" and carries the poet forward
from acceptance of unevent to delighted acknowledg-
ment of an event:

> Be witness that on waking, this mid-winter,
> I found her hand in mine laid closely
> Who shall watch out the Spring with me.
> We stared in silence all around us
> But found no winter anywhere to see.

The years 1938–42 produced only eighteen poems, of
which three were subsequently dropped. Yet there was
no falling away in their quality, rather an increasing
complexity in their detail. Because of the impact of
events, perhaps, Graves ceased to make reference to public themes; nothing is now said about the decay of

civilisation, and even the monsters in whom he had once symbolised the predatory and destructive attitude of burgher society now become almost likable trolls. Certainly his "Lollocks" are kinder and more playful than the ogres and pygmies of a few years before; they are no more than grubby spirits of disorder that can be expelled by a regimen of cleanliness:

> Sovereign against Lollocks
> Are hard broom and soft broom,
> To well comb the hair,
> To well brush the shoe,
> And to pay every debt
> As it falls due.

In the mid-winter of the war, Robert Graves, though best known for his historical reconstructions, still showed great achievement and promise as a poet now chiefly concerned with themes of love.

REFERENCES

1. *G.B.*, p. 23.
2. *G.B.*, pp. 77–8.
3. *G.B.*, p. 30.
4. *G.B.*, pp. 54–5.
5. *G.B.*, p. 85.
6. *Occupation Writer*, pp. 62–79.
7. *G.B.*, p. 79.
8. *G.B.*, p. 37.
9. Foreword to *Poems 1938–45*.
10. *I Claudius*, p. 103.
11. *I.C.*, p. 285.
12. *Claudius the God*, p. 251.
13. *I.C.*, pp. 98–9.
14. *C.G.*, pp. 220–5.
15. *Count Belisarius*, p. 56.
16. *C.B.*, p. 421.
17. *C.B.*, pp. 149–51.
18. *Sergeant Lamb*, p. 118.
19. *Wife to Mr Milton*, p. 151.
20. *O.W.*, pp. 222–40.
21. *C.A.*, pp. 61–167, *passim*.

CHAPTER V

THE WHITE GODDESS:
MYTH AND POETRY

"The myths are wearing thin," wrote Graves, towards
the conclusion of *The White Goddess*, his "historical grammar of poetic myth." "When the English language was
first formed, all educated people were thinking within
the framework of the Christian myth cycle. But now," he
concludes, "Biblical myths no longer serve as a secure
basis of poetic reference. Moreover the Latin and Greek
myths which have always been as important to the poets
(professionally at least) as the Christian, are also losing
their validity." The poet, once a privileged bard who
preserved the religious secrets of the tribe, now dwells in
the wilderness, where "the temptation to monomaniac
raving, paranoia and eccentric behaviour has been too
much for many of the exiles."[1] It behoved a poet, therefore, to invent new myths or to breathe fresh life into the
old. In endeavouring to choose the second alternative,
Graves perhaps in fact chose the first. The mythology of
The White Goddess, though its elements are drawn from a
vast field of ancient story and legend, is in its assemblage
his own creation, and conforms to the requirements of his
own poetic mind.

The discovery of the dilemma was not peculiar to
Graves. Almost every poet in the main English tradition
since the time of Baudelaire had complained that there
was no framework of thought common to himself and his
potential reader. Hence the elaboration by many—
Yeats, Blok, Rilke, George, and Lorca among the chief—
of entirely new symptoms, based on their own private

experience, but advanced as if they possessed a universal validity. Yeats's division of humanity according to the phase of the moon under which an individual was born; Blok's theory of music and of revolution; Rilke's invention of a hierarchy of angels who bore no resemblance to those of theology but stood rather for Platonic ideas; George's myth of the dead redeemer Maximin, and Lorca's cult of the gipsy at feud with the Civil Guard, all were attempts to substitute new myths for old. Graves's attempt seems at first sight more conservative. He has chosen to reinterpret the familiar stories in the Old and New Testament, the legends about the Greek gods and heroes, the Homeric tales, and the histories treated by the Welsh and Irish bards. He claims that his approach is scholarly. Like Yeats he sets out his theory in prose. But Yeats understood that the material expounded in *The Vision*, which derived from his wife's automatic scripts, was primarily poetic rather than cosmological. For the spirits told him at the outset: "We have come to give you metaphors for your poetry." Graves, on the other hand, adopting a show of scholarship and influenced in the first place by Sir James Frazer's powers of assemblage and co-ordination in *The Golden Bough*, advanced his newly interpreted myths as if they were not only a basis for poetry but actual statements of historical truth, hitherto transmitted in disguised form but now for the first time yielding their secret to investigation.

The White Goddess does not stand alone. Such works as Margaret Murray's *God of the Witches* and Hugh Ross Williamson's *The Arrow and The Sword*, which attribute a variety of events in modern history to the survival of pre-Christian rituals, provide obvious parallels. Free and semi-scholarly interpretations of the past have lately seemed to provide an attractive alternative to the narrow scholarship and vast assemblages of facts that characterise many modern histories. To relate all past happenings to the Marxist myth of the class struggle was perhaps excusable; the theory threw some light on the English Civil Wars and the French Revolution. But to elaborate a counter-myth to that of the Mission, Passion, and Resurrection of Jesus Christ, as Graves did, appeared even in the Forties somewhat over-bold.

The novel *King Jesus* is the first of Graves's major re-interpretations. Perhaps the germ for them can be found in the earlier historical novels, in which ancient events were made to conform to modern ideas of psychology, military science, medicine, etc.; and a precedent for this novel certainly exists in George Moore's *Brook Kerith*, in which Jesus was presented as a pupil of the Essenes, who returned to their community after being taken down from the Cross still living. But Moore's concern was with the artistry of his narrative, not with the truth of his theory. In *King Jesus* Graves sets out a hypothesis, which turns all Jewish and Christian traditions completely upside down. The Jesus of his book is not the sacrificed Saviour but the lost heir to the throne of Judah, a preacher absolutely loyal to the Jewish religion. In all his novels so far Graves had put his historical research at the disposal of his story-telling. Now he used his narrative skill to make palatable a curious theory that went counter to all accepted belief.

"To write a novel by the analeptic method," wrote Graves in his historical commentary on *King Jesus*,[2]—the intuitive recovery of forgotten events by a deliberate suspension of time—"one must train oneself to think wholly in contemporary terms." This is most easily done by impersonating the supposed author of the story (as Graves had already done with the Emperor Claudius). His mouthpiece, Agabus the Decapolitan, was not presented as a close contemporary of Jesus. As a detached theoretician, he is able to explain the divergences in the Synoptic tradition, and to comment on Church policy after the fall of Jerusalem. Graves reconstructs the events and reinterprets Jesus's sayings in the light of His belief that He was the rightful King of the Jews, that He was lamed for ritual purposes, that He was born to Mary and Joseph, adopted by the second Mary, a priestess whom we know as Mary Magdalene, and betrothed to the third Mary, the sister of Lazarus. This series of hypotheses, ably argued on the basis of evidence drawn from the most various and incongruous sources, explains to Graves's satisfaction the mystery of the Virgin Birth, the reasons for Pilate's concern with Jesus, for the wording of the inscription above the Cross, and for the manner of His execution. Graves's attitude to the past has now become that of a detective who expects all clues to have been painfully concealed, awaiting his arrival on the scene. He seems in a left-handed way to accept the principle of esotericism, whereby the truth is always preserved by the few and delivered in diluted form to the many, but to attribute popular ignorance rather to a series of mis-understandings than to a purposive adaptation of the truth to the level of their comprehension. The truth of the New Testament story seems to him to lie in a cryptogram which any pertinacious and literal-minded scholar may break down. One factor to which Graves attributes many popular errors is the practice of iconotropy, by which he means the fortuitous misreading of ancient pictures or carvings by new peoples who conquer countries of old civilisation. He believes that they invent literal stories to explain the iconography of their predecessors, and then foist them on the world as history, secular or divine. A hostile critic might accuse Graves of following a similar practice, that of interpreting religious symbolism as if it were a statement of plain facts.

King Jesus was published as a novel and, were its story told of a self-deluded preacher of another name, though less deft than *I Claudius*, it would count as a well-written but rather digressive historical tale. *The White Goddess*, on the other hand, is a piece of exposition devoid of fictional plot, which relies for its dramatic excitement on a

series of reinterpretations of material familiar and un-
familiar, as wayward and revolutionary as Graves's
treatment of the New Testament story, but far more important in the study of his poetry. Less closely patterned
and less consequent than *The Vision*, it is, like Yeats's
book, a quarry of potential imagery for its author.

Graves described the genesis of *The White Goddess* in a
lecture delivered to a New York audience in February
1957, which he printed in the miscellany *Steps*.[3] While
working on his novel, *The Golden Fleece*, he was, it seems,
interrupted by "a sudden overwhelming obsession,"
which took the form of "an unsolicited enlightenment"
on a subject he knew almost nothing of. A night and day
of furious cogitation was followed by three weeks of in-
tense work, during which the whole 70,000 words of the
original version were written. Graves compares his first
intimations of the subject of the mysterious "Battle of the
Trees" with the experience of the chemist Friedrich von
Stradonitz, who had a vision of serpents waltzing round,
tail to mouth, in a ring, and suddenly *knew* what they
meant. He then wrote out his "closed ring" theory of the
constituents of benzene, of which he had so far no proof,
but which was afterwards found to be correct.

Graves's point of departure was the "Song of Taliesin"
in Lady Charlotte Guest's version of *The Mabinogion*, an
apparently nonsensical minstrel poem which, he decided,
must have been deliberately coded or "pied" and which
he related by intuitive reasoning with the ancient poetic
tradition of "The Battle of the Trees," mentioned in the
notes of *The Mabinogion*. These two Welsh texts, he further decided, would only make sense in the light of an
ancient Irish religious and poetic tradition. Though
neither a Welsh nor an Irish scholar, he proceeded to
restore the lines to their original order. From this point
the book's argument wanders from Wales to Greece and
then back to Ireland, interpreting folklore, examining
the attributes of gods, and constructing etymologies that

link the Middle East with the furthest West. In the process "must," "might," "seem," and other verbs of hypothesis yield on the basis of dubious authorities to "is" and
"have." Herodotus, Plutarch and many more modern
theorists are drawn on. But the work is never for a
moment a work of scholarship. It was not conceived as
such. Digressive, poetic and allusive, it can compare only
with that seventeenth-century masterpiece, Burton's
Anatomy of Melancholy, which enriched the stock of English
poetic imagery, and proved a valuable source book to
the Romantics.

Beginning as a piece of curiously inspired investigation
into the history of myth, *The White Goddess* becomes in its
final chapters a tract for the age. After tracing the pattern
of spiritual and cultural disasters which has reduced
poetry to its present low state, Graves proceeds to attack
the various fashionable schools. By their obscurity, he
says, present-day surrealists, impressionists, expression-
ists, and neo-romantics are only "concealing their un-
happy lack of a secret."[4] To preserve the secret of a people
was, in Graves's belief, the task of poets in the great ages
of the past. But now he can see no change for the better
until things have become much worse. The remedy lies
in the revival of goddess-worship, the reversion from
patriarchal to matriarchal society, and the abandonment
of cold intellectuality, which Graves associates with
perversion.

The main theme of poetry, in his belief, should be the
relations of man and woman, and for the poet there is no
other woman but Cerridwen (The White Sow Goddess)
who alone is independent of the male magician.

Other women, other goddesses are kinder-seeming.
They sell their love at a reasonable rate—sometimes a
man may even have it for the asking. But not Cerridwen: for with her love goes wisdom . . .

Cerridwen abides. Poetry began in the matriarchal

age, and derives its magic from the moon, not from the sun. No poet can hope to understand the nature of poetry unless he has had a vision of the Naked King crucified to the lopped oak, and watched the dancers, red-eyed from the acrid smoke of the sacrificial fires, stamping out the measure of the dance, their bodies bent uncouthly forward, with a monotonous chant of: "Kill! kill! kill!" and "Blood! blood! blood!"

Constant illiterate use of the phrase "to woo the Muse" has obscured its poetic sense: the poet's inner communion with the White Goddess, regarded as the source of truth.[5]

Graves had moved from the romanticism of his nursery-rhyme poems to the negatively classical restraint of his poetry of the Thirties. The result seemed to be an emotional impoverishment that was transforming his work into a formal exercise. New romanticism was accepted again in the name of the White Goddess. The wells of unconscious belief and association could be re-opened without the need immediately to dilute their waters with the acid of self-criticism and doubt. While Graves certainly fails satisfactorily to reinterpret the myths of the past, *The White Goddess* in its wayward exposition of his own deepest experience tells of a new freedom and a new source of power. Such a poem as "The Love Story" requires no theoretical exposition to interpret its images. Even if some are obscure they explain themselves by reference to the poem as a whole. The context of a particular image in Graves's thought can often be explained by reference to his theories. His discovery of the goddess, however, was not the result of deciphering obscure poems. Suddenly his powers of emotion, long damned, became free. The writing of *The White Goddess* was one result of this release. Another and more vital consequence was a new burst of poetry concerning the postulated theme, the relations of man and woman.

As a pendant to *The White Goddess*, Graves wrote his
two-volume compendium of *The Greek Myths*, which was
published by Penguin Books in 1955. The myths themselves are recounted in sound, simple prose, and each is
divided into sections according to the various sources of
its often contradictory details. There had been no collection of this kind since the mid-nineteenth century and, so
far as the narrative is concerned, the collection is successful. Graves's interpretations, however, are somewhat
wayward. He believes that "a large part of Greek myth
is politico-religious history,"[6] and that it is principally
concerned with the matters that were the main subject
of *The White Goddess*. Matriarchy, the changing relations
between the matriarchal queen and her lovers, the moon
and the moon calendar, feature so largely in his explana-
tory notes that there is no room for any psychological or
mystical connotations which they may possess. The adjec-
tive "religious" appears to have for him in this context a
purely sociological meaning. In dealing with Orpheus,
for instance, he barely mentions the Mysteries; the
symbolism of the musician's descent into hell is ignored.
But Orpheus's power of making the trees dance is instantly associated with the theme of the tree alphabet
expounded in *The White Goddess*. Graves, in fact, is quick
to bring out those features in a myth which chime with
his beliefs, and to support his case with proofs drawn from
a very wide and various reading.

Another feature of Orpheus story that engages Graves's
attention is his dismemberment by the Maenads, which
associates him with Dionysus and ancient poetry. For the
Maenads represent the Muses, whose promiscuity he is
said to have condemned, at the same time preaching the
virtues of homosexual love. Thus he incurred the anger
of Aphrodite as well as of Apollo.[7] But, according to
Graves, Orpheus was also like Jesus an incarnation of the
Sacred King. This lack of balance leads him almost entirely to ignore the Eurydice story, which throws no

light on his theories. He explains it away as an icono-tropical misunderstanding of a picture of Orpheus's descent into the underworld. The invading Greeks, it seems, mistook the Pelasgian snake goddess Hecate, who was shown among the gods receiving him, for a mortal woman who had been bitten by a snake. They then invented the figure of Orpheus's lost wife to explain her presence, and presumably embellished their invention with the tale of her conditional release and his backward glance.

Graves's telling of the myths is simple, though sometimes a little over-detailed in the matter of presumed geographical location. An excerpt from his version of the Orpheus legend telling of Eurydice's death shows his power of writing plain prose without taint of pastiche:

> One day, near Tempe, in the valley of the river Peneius, Eurydice met Aristaeus, who tried to force her. She trod on a serpent as she fled, and died of its bite; but Orpheus boldly descended into Tartarus, hoping to fetch her back. He used the passage that opens at Aornus in Thesprotis and, on his arrival, not only charmed the ferryman Charon, the dog Cerberus, and the three Judges of the Dead, with his plaintive music, but temporarily suspended the tortures of the damned; and so far soothed the savage heart of Hades that he won leave to restore Eurydice to the upper world. . . .[8]

How much is being held back can be seen by comparison with such a poem as Rilke's "Orpheus, Eurydike, Hermes" or with Graves's own almost entirely translated "Instructions to the Orphic Adept":

> After your passage through Hell's seven floods,
> Whose fumes of sulphur will have parched your throat,
> The Halls of Judgment shall loom up before you,
> A miracle of jasper and of onyx.

> To the left hand there bubbles a black spring
> Overshadowed with a great white cypress.
> Avoid this spring, which is Forgetfulness;
> Though all the common rout rush down to drink,
> Avoid this spring.

In his version of this Greek text, which is partially translated from tablets that are more likely to be Pythagorean than Orphic, Graves shows a far deeper understanding of the legend than his bald prose account of it would suggest. He knows that the descent into hell in fact represents the initiation of an adept, and that he must rightfully be taken as a mystery god, the very opposite of the homosexual enemy of the Maenads described in the *Myths*. Moreover the "Orphic" poem dwells on the ideas of remembering and forgetting in a way that shows deep psychological understanding. Graves the poet and translator understands many things that are hidden from Graves the inventor of theories. The adept on descending into the underworld,

> Out of the weary wheel, the circling years,
> To that still, spokeless wheel,

is offered the draught of forgetfulness from the spring beneath the cypress. If he drinks of it, he will forget that he is a man of Samothrace, and when he returns to earth he will forget his experience of this other world, as do "the common rout" of those who come down to Tartarus. But the purpose of this initiation, which brings with it a moment of higher consciousness, is that it shall be remembered. Therefore the adept must drink of the serpent-guarded spring of remembrance beneath the hazel. Then he will remember Samothrace, and will become lord over

> the uninitiated
> Twittering ghosts, Hell's countless populace.

The poem's statement is similar to those which are found in the Platonic myths, in the Egyptian and in the Tibetan Book of the Dead. The original symbolism, however, which Graves's poem does not convey, related this initiation to the leaving of the body at the moment of death, when forgetfulness overcomes "the common rout," and the retention of consciousness brings with it release from "the weary wheel" of repeated lives. This meaning is present in the other three texts mentioned.

Graves's prose works since the last of the historical reconstructions, *Wife to Mr Milton*, include in addition to *King Jesus*; a retelling of the tale of Jason, *The Golden Fleece*; an account of a Spanish voyage of discovery to the Solomon Islands in the year 1595, entitled *The Isles of Unwisdom*; and *Homer's Daughter*, a fictional development of Samuel Butler's theory that the *Odyssey* was written by a woman. In the last-named, which is probably the most interesting of the three, he works out a theory almost as bold as that of *King Jesus* or *The White Goddess*, which advances the writing of the epic by three hundred years, and identifies its author as the Princess Nausicaa of the modern Trapani in Sicily. His attitude to the *Odyssey* has always been perverse. In reviewing T. E. Lawrence's translation[9] he maintained, perhaps half in fun, that to be successful it should have been modelled on some such work as Charlotte Brontë's tale, *The Spell*, which she wrote at the age of eighteen. He even argued that Lawrence sometimes came near to this style. For the *Iliad*, on the other hand he chooses Malory as the translator who would best have been able to reproduce "its proper, semi-barbaric flavour." His own version of 1960, however, *The Anger of Achilles*, follows the very different example of the Welsh or Irish bards. His translation is almost entirely in prose. But he resorts to somewhat jingling verse at those moments when he believes prose will not suffice. While his narrative prose is pleasantly contemporary, there is little to suggest that either Homer or his

translator had "derived magic from the moon" before
describing the death of Patroclus at the hands of Hector
in these words:

> A lion sprang at a wild boar
>   When, crazed with cruel thirst,
> Beside a mountain spring they met
>   And each would drink at first;
> It was the stalwart lion's luck
>   That panting boar to worst!

Graves finds satirical intentions in the *Iliad*. But such
verses suggest the downright impatience that he felt with
the Latin poet Lucan, whose *Pharsalia* he put into prose
as a Penguin Classic. His versions of *The Golden Ass* and
of Suetonius's *Twelve Caesars*, one of his chief source-
books for the Claudius novels, are, however, consum-
mate adaptations. No one has been more successful than
Graves in the translation of elaborate Latin into brisk
contemporary English.

Graves's poetry since his contribution to *Work in
Progress* in the middle of the Second World War fills a
little more than the last third of the 1959 volume, into
which it was collected from three small books and the
concluding section of the miscellany *Steps*. From these
volumes very few pieces were subsequently discarded; in
fact many quite trivial pieces have been retained. The
opening lines of "Mid-winter Waking," a poem already
quoted in the last chapter, might serve as epigraph to
them all:

> Stirring suddenly from long hibernation,
> I knew myself once more a poet
> Guarded by timeless principalities
> Against the worm of death, this hillside haunting;
> And presently dared open both my eyes.

Graves's hibernation had never been complete. He had
always kept one poetic eye open. But once the two sides of

his production began to draw together, once his prose interest was in poetic material (although he did not always interpret it poetically), and a part of his casual writing took the form of light poems, something new came into his poetry. The emotion which had been missing since his nursery-rhyme period, and which had been rejected whenever it attempted to appear, now emerged in greater strength than ever.

Graves's later poetry, whether it refers obliquely to an actual incident or relates it in the form of a myth, is all love poetry. In this, reason plays the part of commentator upon feeling. Often it affects to see further than feeling, and often it speaks apprehensively. But now the brain no longer impedes the heart. Graves has brought his work into balance, and the reconciling factor, no doubt a personal one which is not directly expressed in the poetry, would seem to have worked this miracle while he was writing the last poems to be included in his small volume *Poems 1938–45*. The change is first evident in "Mid-winter Waking" of 1939.

Among the poems in this volume that had not already appeared four years before in *Work in Hand* five are outstanding: two love poems of exceptional lucidity, "Through Nightmare" and "The Door"; a poem in honour of a child, "To Lucia at Birth"; the mythological "Theseus and Ariadne"; and the magical "To Juan at the Winter Solstice."

"Through Nightmare" speaks of a depth of insight or vision in a loved woman that the poet envies and admires, and that he sees has not been attained easily, since it can only be approached "through nightmare" by one "timorous by nature." The poem is a tribute to the feminine mind that is unaffected by history and makes straight for the truth:

> The untameable, the live, the gentle.
> Have you not known them? Whom? They carry

Time looped so river-wise about their house
There's no way in by history's road
To name or number them.

The "Lost or moated land" in which she dwells,
"lying at large remove beyond all dream" contains the
answer to the questions of such a nihilistic poem as "The
Castle," (a genuine nightmare which, as Graves records,
was only dissolved by accidentally visiting the place itself,
Berry Pomeroy Castle in Devon). The poet is no longer
compelled to believe that "There is no escape, no such
thing." The way out of time is seen to lead to a visionary
state near to the still centre where a man is surrounded
and yet unaffected by time. The discovery has already
been made in the "Orphic" translation. The experience
described in "The Terraced Valley" is now not argued
away but accepted on behalf of another person. "The
untameable," once thought of as ogres, pygmies, or at best
playful lollocks, but in any case elementals, are now seen
to be also "the live" and "the gentle." It is their company
that is to be found on the further side of dream.

In "The Door" also it is the woman that introduces the
deepest experience, in this case symbolised by the arche-
typal "visiting sea," which is admitted to the poet's room
when she enters and again shut out as she departs. The
advance from "Mid-winter Waking" is considerable, but
that from such an early poem as the self-regarding "Lost
Love" is very much greater, since now the poet finds pro-
founder reality in the loved woman than in himself.

The lesson that reality lies not inside but outside time,
that events cannot be controlled, but inner attitudes to
them can, is driven home in "To Lucia at Birth." In it
the moon is shown under two aspects, "matronly and
bland" and menacing. Graves's cortège of war and
disaster is more deeply apprehended than his former
nihilistic visions of the doom of civilisation. There is both
warning and comfort in the lines:

Outrageous company to be born into,
   Lunatics of a royal rage long dead.
Then reckon time by what you are or do
   Not by the epochs of the war they spread.
   Hark how they roar; but never turn your head,
Nothing will change them, let them not change you.

It is significant that the poem is addressed to a girl-child. For in woman, whether as goddess, wife, or girl Graves now finds all the positive attitudes of which he despaired in the past.

"Theseus and Ariadne," the rehandling of a myth that perhaps contains private applications, also endows woman with the deeper insight, proving the hero mistaken and self-deluded. It is a successor to "Alice," a study in reality and illusion, or in two different realities, that of the mind and that of the world. Theseus has deserted Ariadne, who showed him the way into the Cretan maze and gave him the thread by which he escaped after slaying the Minotaur. Now married to a new queen, he dreams of her as she was when he left her, thinking of her palace as fallen with time to "rubble and rank grass." The first six lines describe Theseus's dream, in which he sees her as still the woman he knew, and still sunk in his "erroneous past." In fact Ariadne, whom Graves believes to have been yet one more incarnation of the white Moon Goddess,[10] did not die deserted in childbirth on the shores of Cyprus, as one version of the myth tells, but returned to marry her rightful husband, the Cretan Dionysus. So not only is Theseus's imagination contrasted with the truth about Ariadne, but one version of the myth is made to contradict the other. For though Theseus remembers Ariadne, she has forgotten him:

   And with a surer foot she goes than when
   Dread of his hate was thunder in the air,
   When the pines agonized with flaws of wind

> And flowers gazed up at her with frantic eyes.
> Of him, now all is done, she never dreams . . .

Her agony was in the past, when she dreaded his leaving her, but he imagines it to be in the present; he sees her in shadows, but in fact she is

> Playing the queen to nobler company

to a god instead of to a king.

Graves's explanation of Theseus's desertion of Ariadne in the notes to his version of the Myth are on a strangely lower level of insight. It would seem that in fact he did not abandon her till they came to the last island in the Cretan world. Since even as a queen she could not transfer her rights from the matrilinear world of Crete to patrilinear Athens, Theseus acted from political motives or self-interest.[11]

The same theme of alternate aspects of the truth is repeated in two light and ironic poems, "Dream of a Climber" and "The Persian Version," the first of which tells of the climber's pose in full mountaineering kit on the lowest rung of his ladder, only to be portrayed in the newspaper next day

> nearly out of view, almost in the cloud,
> Leaning aside for an angel to pass,

while the other gives an allegedly Persian account of "the trivial skirmish fought near Marathon," in which, in language that parodies that of official battle communiqués,

> Despite a strong defence and adverse weather
> All arms combined magnificently together.

"To Juan at the Winter Solstice," by contrast, denying all contradictions, states that every legend is in fact a version of the one legend. This is the conclusion to which Graves came in writing *The White Goddess*. Here all myths are shown to have a single meaning, and all goddesses, whatever their names or lands, to be one. Whether she is Isis, Aphrodite, or the Irish Grainne, whether mourning for the murder of Osiris, Tammuz, Adonis, or Diarmuid, at the hands of Set, or Apollo, or Finn MacCool,[12] always it is the same murder in October, the boar-hunting season; always it is the death of the Sacred King who is to be reborn at the winter solstice. It is perhaps as Aphrodite, who rose from the sea, that Graves sees her in these lines from "To Juan":

> Dwell on her graciousness, dwell on her smiling,
> Do not forget what flowers
> The great boar trampled down in ivy time.
> Her brow was creamy as the crested wave,
> Her sea-blue eyes were wild
> But nothing promised that was not performed.

The poem contains many references to *The White Goddess* sometimes most cryptically coded.

> Water to water, ark again to ark,
> From woman back to woman:
> So each new victim treads unfalteringly
> The never altered circuit of his fate,
> Bringing twelve peers as witness
> Both to his starry rise and starry fall.

This sequence, *water*, *ark*, *woman* (actually Egyptian), is interpreted by the light of Graves's belief that the ancient Arkites, listed in Genesis x, were in fact worshippers of the Moon Goddess Astarte,[13] who now takes Aphrodite's place. The twelve peers and the ever renewed and identical sacrifice seem to refer to the death of Osiris and to the scattering of his twelve limbs, which Isis recovers in her boat, also to the Twelve Knights of the Round Table and the Twelve Peers of France,[14] who in their turn stand for the twelve months of the year. For Graves's preoccupation with the "tree calendar" is also reflected in this poem.

"To Juan at the Winter Solstice" depends as much as anything by Yeats on an understanding of the mythology behind it. For this reason, although packed with magnificent imagery and majestic in its sweep, it cannot count among Graves's finest poems.

"Lament for Pasiphaë" also, another classical piece in this group, can only be fully understood by reference to Graves's interpretations of the myths. Only in this context will the significance of the dying sun in its first line become clear:

Dying sun, shine warm a little longer.

For Pasiphaë, the wife of King Minos, who loved a bull and bore the Minotaur, here appears as the moon goddess who has been married to the sun. The theory is set out in the notes to the myth of Minos and his Brothers.[15]

Unlike the poem "To Juan," this "Lament" is constructed on two levels of meaning. Clearly it refers not only to the mythical queen but to some living woman seen as her counterpart. In this second context the sun may stand, in the manner of Yeats, for the poet himself and his "ageing heart." The poem, however, even when read in this dual light, retains its obscurities; the image of "Spring's Cuckoo with bedraggled plumes" refers, as Graves explains, to Zeus's epiphany to Hera, who took pity on him and got raped. Two other pieces which appear in the text of *The White Goddess* and are reprinted in the 1959 collection remain obscure. Neither "The Destroyer" nor "Return of the Goddess" yields the clue to its symbolism even by reference to the "grammar of poetic myth" to which it is apparently related.

Graves's next small volume, *Poems and Satires 1951*, contains in addition to a piece or two from *The White Goddess* and some pleasant trifles, four poems which testify to a new extension of the poet's talents.

One of these, "Darien," though it contains some images only to be understood in the light of *The White Goddess*, advances beyond them, to significances private to Graves's own mythology, and the other three ignore the goddess myth altogether.

In "Darien," however, the Muse is identified with Aphrodite the Moon Goddess, "presaged by the darting halcyon bird," the building of whose nest, which floated on the water, "evidently refers to the birth of the new Sacred King, at the winter solstice."[16] Furthermore, she is made to carry a Cretan axe, the instrument with which she kills the king of the old year.[17] But the name Darien, given to the future son of the poet and his Muse, clearly belongs to some new symbolism personal to him. It may be a child's name, and it may also stand for the poetry to be born to him after the sacrifice of his old self, the incarnation of the departing year. The poem's conclusion contains some obscure images, but its general meaning is not enigmatic. The poet assumes the role of the king about to be slain:

> I knew then by the trembling of her hands
> For whom that flawless blade would sweep:
> My own oracular head, swung by its hair.
>
> 'Mistress,' I cried, 'the times are evil
> And you have charged me with their remedy.
> O, where my head is now, let nothing be
> But a clay counterfeit with nacre blink:
> Only look up, so Darien may be born.
>
> 'He is the northern star, the spell of knowledge,
> Pride of all hunters and all fishermen,
> Your deathless fawn, an eaglet of your eyrie,
> The topmost branch of your unfellable tree,
> A tear streaking the summer night,
> The new green of my hope.'
>   Lifting her eyes,
> She held mine for a lost eternity.
> 'Sweetheart,' said I, 'strike now, for Darien's sake!'

The old head will be replaced by a mask, perhaps the prophetic mask, for the former oracular office of the poet is frequently referred to in *The White Goddess*; at the same time the severed head, like that of Orpheus[18] will speak oracles.

At the end of the poem the shift to nature imagery suggests that the goddess has now assumed the form of Diana. Darien stands thus for the child foreknown, and the rebirth of the middle-aged poet by sacrifice of the self to this figure of Muse, huntress, goddess, and sweetheart in one.

The second outstanding poem in the 1951 volume, "The Young Cordwainer," bears some resemblance to Keats's "La belle Dame sans Merci," a poem which Graves has related to Keats's circumstances at the time of its composition, the lady standing for love in the person of Fanny Brawne, death by consumption, and the Muse or spirit of poetry, which seemed to have deserted him. A further reference which Graves makes to the White Goddess herself must be taken as somewhat too forced a concession to an overriding interest.[19]

"The Young Cordwainer" is an attempt to build up a scheme of multiple symbolisms like that of Keats, on an equally traditional theme. A masterpiece of carefully contrived compression, it succeeds, like other poems of this period, even when the images are not perfectly understood.

The source of the dialogue between the young shoemaker and the beautiful lady is a mysterious old French ballad, which Graves printed in *The White Goddess*,[20] and which he very boldly interpreted as in origin a conversation between the Welsh god Llew Law and the Moon Goddess. In analysing it, however, in this strange light, he decided that the speaking parts of the lady and the shoemaker had been exchanged. In his poem he follows his own interpretation, leaving the initiative with the young shoemaker up to the last moment when he has lured her, apparently fearful and unwilling, into the tower chamber where she will have him slain by his rival. Up to the last she falters:

> Love, have you the password,
>   Or have you the key,
> With a sharp naked sword
>   And wine to revive me?

But even as he enters he knows himself to be doomed

> Enter; here is starlight,
>   Here the state bed
> Where your man lies all night
>   With blue flowers garlanded.

The blue flower is the periwinkle, which symbolises death. For the lady will bind him to the bedpost, and drug him with the wine that he has brought, once he has satisfied her waning desires, symbolised earlier in the poem by a primrose. In the French ballad the river (of death) passes through the bed, a river so broad that all the king's horses could drink from it at the same time. The poem ends with the lady at the window awaiting the completion of the action.

"The Young Cordwainer" recaptures much of the simplicity of Graves's nursery-rhyme ballads. It has the beauty of fairy-tale. He himself associates it by a series of assumptions with a whole field of mythology. Indeed without recourse to *The White Goddess* the actual meaning of the story would be obscure, and even in the light of the French ballad and the poet's interpretation of it, not every image falls into place.

"The Survivor," another outstanding poem in the 1951 volume, while taking up the old theme of the poet's survival from war as almost the last of his generation, doubles the theme of ordeal by war with another of ordeal by love—"the double suicide (Heart against Heart)"—and asks whether after eluding those "hags,

the spoilers of the field"—a reference perhaps to scenes
of body-snatching in Apuleius—a man can know real joy:

> Is this joy? to be doubtless alive again,
> And the others dead? Will your nostrils gladly savour
> The fragrance, always new, of a first hedge-rose?
> Will your ears be charmed by the thrush's melody
> Sung as if he had himself devised it?

The question is asked in different forms in each of the
poem's three verses, and the implied answer is that,
though to survive the war may bring some shadow of joy,
none can survive the "double suicide" of a broken love.

"Darien," "The Young Cordwainer," and "The
Survivor" mark a succession of splendid stages in an
advance towards independence of interpreted myth, and
the revived power to clothe fresh experience in its own
imagery. The next small volume of *Poems 1953*, the
hitherto uncollected pieces in the 1959 volume, and a few
that since appeared in periodicals, carry this process a
little further forward, but mark no considerable advance
on the best pieces in *Poems 1951*. Satires and grotesques,
mostly contributed in the first place to the *New Yorker*,
predominate. Some still deriving their themes from *The
White Goddess* present problems of meaning that can be at
least partially resolved by reference to that "grammar of
myth." But a few stand out for the directness of their
statements and the patient honesty of their reasoning.
The sole theme new—or almost new—to the 1953
volume is that of personal foreboding. The love poems
now tell, more insistently even than "Lament for Pasiphaë," of enjoyment beneath the shadow of disaster. The
poet may ask too much; the woman may be frightened
by his very insistence.

In "The Foreboding" the poet sees his own weird or
double in the act of writing his mistress's name on some
future day after she has deserted him. "Dialogue on the
Headland" is spoken by two lovers who outbid one an-

other in protestations, yet are always haunted by the possible significance of the phrase in their oaths, "Whatever happens," and jealous of the loves and landscapes in each others' past. "The Straw" speaks of the doom, divined by a straw carried in the poet's fingers, that must always attend requited love:

> Requited love; but better unrequited
> If this chance instrument give warning
> Of cataclysmic agony far away.
> Were she at ease, warmed by the thought of me,
> Would not my hand stay steady as this rock?
> Have I undone her by my vehemence?

"Dethronement," the most important poem in the 1953 collection to treat a theme from *The White Goddess*, portrays the poet as pursued by his own Muse, an Actaeon chased by the hounds of Diana, and condemned to run even though he knows that if he could allow himself to be devoured he would find peace. Yet he can only urge himself on:

> Run, though you hope for nothing: to stay your foot
> Would be ingratitude, a sour denial
> That the life she bestowed was sweet.
> Therefore be fleet, run gasping, draw the chase
> Up the grand defile.

Though here Graves may believe that his "true anguish is all that she requires," in "The Face in the Mirror" he is still ready, like a young man, "to court the queen," whether Muse or mistress, "in her high silk pavilion," and in "Spoils" he triumphantly affirms that whereas what is won in war may be sold anonymously, the spoils of love never grow cold. The portrait presented is of a man who knows the worst, yet has preserved a young heart.

Perhaps Graves's heart was late in finding its freedom. Certainly even the slightest of the late poems possess an

emotional quality that was absent in the more intellectual and thwarted poetry of his middle years. Even his
prophecies of doom are muted; if a breakdown of civilisation is foreseen it is with some compassion and a little
distant hope. Nor is Graves now the savage critic of any
institution, except that of half-love cemented by the
marriage bond. "With Her Lips Only," "A Slice of
Wedding Cake," and "Call It a Good Marriage," three
light and accomplished poems, all make the same protest. The wheel of his thoughts has made a full revolution,
and personal values have completely reasserted themselves.

Self-portraiture also, since the conclusion of his autobiography an involuntary feature only in Graves's
writing, is no longer eschewed. Not only does he declare
his feelings about love and approaching old age, he even
attempts in "The Second Fated," the outstanding poem
in the final section of the 1959 collection, to give a sketch
of his life seen as a whole.

> Fortune enrolled me among the second-fated
> Who have read their own obituaries in *The Times*,

he proclaims, reverting once more to the theme of un-
expected survival, and more particularly perhaps, to the
fact that his name was once included in the casualty lists
as killed in France. The reputation of Graves the poet has
indeed suffered a premature death followed by a strong
revival. In the poem's opening lines he renounces that
one of his post-war selves who played with "the metaphysical idiom" that he is now reluctant to use. He is one
of those "certain few" who are unsatisfied by any
accepted account of the universe

> formed scientifically
> From whatever there was before Time was.

Speaking for these few who have fallen under the influence of the Mother Goddess and Muse, and have made

the descent into the shades with Orpheus and returned to
the upper world, he proclaims himself free to beg "the
question of perfect consequence" and accept a "world of
discontinuance." It is on this note that the poem ends:

> We, to be plain with you, taking advantage
> Of a brief demise, visited first the Pit,
> A library of shades, completed characters;
> And next the silver-bright Hyperborean Queendom,
> Basking under the sceptre of Guess Whom?
> Where pure souls matrilineally foregather.
> We were then shot through by merciful lunar shafts
> Until hearts tingled, heads sang, and praises flowed;
> And learned to scorn your factitious universe
> Ruled by the death which we had flouted;
> Acknowledging only that from the Dove's egg hatched
> Before aught was, but wind—unpredictable
> As our second birth would be, or our second love:
> A moon-warmed world of discontinuance.

The poet has won through, and the reader can feel
confident that the poetry of his old age will be richer than
that of his middle years. For now he has accepted his
own nature, more emotional than intellectual, and understood his own experience. If we see his descent into
hell as standing not for the years of trench warfare when
his feelings were alive or even for the moment of his presumed death from wounds, but for that dry period of self-
thwarting intellectualism that followed the completion of
Good-bye to All That and ended only during the Second
World War, we can with him be grateful for his emergence. Now in his best poems we find the reflexion of real
and personal experience on a brightly polished and recep-
tive mind. Every poet's world is essentially his own abstract
from that other which

> May satisfy the general run of men . . .
> But does not satisfy certain few else. . . ,

and which is ruled over by that death of the spirit from which Graves has arisen as one of the "second-fated." It is possible to see the whole trajectory of his poetry as a struggle to find, know, and accept the power of love; as a battle between the head and the heart in which the heart at first prevailed though without self-knowledge, in which the head for many years overwhelmed it with barren argumentation and disbelief, and in which the heart finally reasserted itself under the somewhat fanciful standard of the Moon Goddess.

Even to the last Graves's is not the poetry of peaceable love. He is no Patmore. Such poems as "Dethronement" and "The Straw" point, as has been said, to a recurrent foreboding that love consumes the lover, and that possession is inevitably followed by loss or betrayal. Perhaps the supreme virtue for him is naturalness obtained by the conscious rejection of all falsity. One must swear no oaths that involve the use of the fatal qualification "Whatever happens"; one must use no words of protestation that "carry a curse with them." It is for these virtues that he praises his beloved most highly in "Forbidden Words," one of the most characteristic of his last poems. That she does not use them "unless ironically in truth's defence," is, he tells her,

> among your several holds on my heart;
> For you are no uninstructed child of Nature,
> But passed in schools and attained the laurel wreath:
> Only to trample it on Apollo's floor.

Graves long ago swore an oath to poetry which he has consistently kept for more than forty-five years. Technically he achieved his full powers as long ago as "Rocky Acres" and "The Pier Glass." Today the lightest of his occasional pieces has a seemingly effortless perfection of cadence and phrase, though, like the nursery-rhyme poems of forty years ago, it is no doubt the product of four or five drafts. No contemporary poet is a greater master of cadence, none more capable of achieving variety within a uniform verse pattern. Nor is there any with greater control of rhyme and half-rhyme, assonance and alliteration. His language is contemporary yet traditional; it calls no attention to itself, and is seldom either over-colloquial or self-important. His theme is the universal relationship of man and woman, poet and Muse. When he rehandles an old myth, he gives it, despite his theoretical attitude, a new meaning; "Theseus and Ariadne" and "Lament for Pasiphaë," as well as other poems of this kind to which I have called no attention, can be read independently of *The White Goddess*, even though that book throws light on their imagery.

In his treatment of myths Graves resembles Rilke and Edwin Muir among his contemporaries, both of whom have endowed old legends with fresh psychological interpretations. He is however a poet of lesser reach than the poet of the *Duineser Elegien*, who was not content to accept a "world of discontinuance" but endeavoured to interpret all experience afresh in his myth of the angels. It is rather with Muir that he stands, though Muir is always the more classical poet, concerned with the great commonplaces of faith and doubt, goodness and evil.

Like any poet who survives to maturity still alive in all his powers, Graves is exercising a beneficient influence on young poets, less direct than that which he exerted on his fellow contributors to *Work in Hand* eighteen years ago. Yet in tightness of organisation, free use of old forms, and meticulous expression he has stood as an incorruptible exemplar to those poets who have emerged in the Fifties in strong reaction against the untidy neo-Romanticism of the previous decade. The work of Philip Larkin, Thom Gunn, Brian Giles, Geoffrey Hill, and Anthony Thwaite, who seem likely to be the leading poets of the Sixties, would all be different and certainly less accomplished if Robert Graves did not stand in the line of their poetic ancestry.

REFERENCES

1. *W.G.*, p. 450.
2. *King Jesus*, p. 353.
3. *S.*, pp. 86–105.
4. *W.G.*, p. 454.
5. *W.G.*, pp. 445–6.
6. *Greek Myths*, I, p. 17.
7. *G.M.*, I, pp. 112–13.
8. *G.M.*, I, p. 112.
9. *S.*, pp. 185–7.
10. *G.M.*, I, p. 347.
11. Ibid.
12. *W.G.*, p. 209.
13. *W.G.*, pp. 143–4.
14. *W.G.*, p. 200.
15. *G.M.*, I, p. 297.
16. *W.G.*, p. 185.
17. *G.M.*, I, p. 297.
18. *G.M.*, I, p. 113.
19. *W.G.*, pp. 425–30.
20. *W.G.*, pp. 321–3.

BIBLIOGRAPHY

Note

*In all cases in which more than one edition of any work is listed, all references in the text are to the edition marked * in this Bibliography*

I. PRINCIPAL WORKS OF ROBERT GRAVES

1. Poetry

Over the Brazier. London 1916.
Fairies and Fusiliers. London 1917, New York 1918.
Country Sentiment. London 1920, New York 1920.
The Pier Glass. London 1921, New York 1921.
Whipperginny. London 1922.
Poems 1914-1926. Contains a full selection from the volumes already mentioned and from some smaller and later ones. London 1927.
Poems 1926–1930. London 1931.
Poems 1930–1933. London 1933.
Collected Poems 1914–1938. London 1938, New York 1939.
Poems 1938–1945. London 1946, New York 1946.
Collected Poems 1914–1947. London 1949.
Poems and Satires 1951. London 1951.
Poems 1953. London 1953.
Robert Graves: Poems Selected by Himself. Makes a very satisfactory introduction to his work. Penguin Poets. Harmondsworth 1957.
Collected Poems 1959. London 1959.

2. Autobiography

Good-bye to All That. London 1929; * Penguin edn., Harmondsworth 1960.

3. Novels

I Claudius. London 1934; * Penguin edn., Harmondsowrth 1941.
Claudius the God. London 1934; * Penguin edn., Harmondsworth 1943.
Count Belisarius. London 1938; * Penguin edn., Harmondsworth 1955.
Wife to Mr Milton. London 1943; * Penguin edn., Harmondsworth 1954.
King Jesus. London 1946; second edition 1960. New York 1956.
Homer's Daughter. London 1955, New York 1955.

4. Criticism

Poetic Unreason. London 1925.
The Common Asphodel. A collection of early critical works. London 1949.

The Crowning Privilege. The Clark Lectures 1954–5, and some
  miscellaneous essays. London 1955; * Penguin edn., Harmondsworth 1959.

5. Mythology

The White Goddess. London 1948, New York 1948; * second edn.,
  amended and enlarged, London 1952.
The Greek Myths. Harmondsworth 1955.

6. Miscellanies

Occupation Writer. Includes revised version of **Lars Porsena and Mrs.
  Fisher.** London 1951.
Steps. London 1958.

II. OTHERS

Little has been written about Robert Graves except in the form of
book-reviews. A pioneer essay on his poetry by Ronald Hayman
appeared in *Essays in Criticism* . v (Jan. 1955), and there is a British
Council pamphlet by Martin Seymour-Smith.